Praise for *Higher Ambition*

"In our book, *In Search of Excellence*, Tom Peters and I wrote that great leaders and managers make meanings for people—not just money. This carefully researched and well-written book explains how 36 CEOs across three continents do just that. Leading with *higher ambition* is not just an option but a necessity for success in tomorrow's corporate world."

—Bob Waterman, coauthor, *In Search of Excellence*; author, *The Renewal Factor, Adhocracy,* and *What America Does Right*

"Businesses must earn from society the right to exist for the long term. The ideas of the CEOs profiled in this book are an invaluable guide to business leaders as they look to practice the right corporate leadership. These ideas will help a new generation of leaders become better CEOs."

—Kris Gopalakrishnan, CEO and cofounder, Infosys Technologies

"The authors provide the first true action guide to creating economic and social value in the global economy. This book moves way beyond the abstract descriptions of organizational attributes in much of today's management literature to concrete discussions of the leadership behaviors necessary to create the world we are hoping to live in. A tour de force that should be carefully read by leaders of all kinds of organizations striving to meet the stakeholder challenges of a new order. Bravo!"

—Leonard A. Schlesinger, President, Babson College; former Vice Chairman and Chief Operating Officer, Limited Brands

"*Higher Ambition* stimulates a long-overdue dialogue about the connection between employees engaged in significant work they are proud to do and the performance of the companies they work for. If you want to lead an organization today and you don't think this matters, I would bet on the success of your competitor."

—Brad Anderson, former CEO and Vice Chairman, Best Buy

"The authors offer a landmark study of leaders and firms that are built on the premise of creating value—not simply extracting it. At a time when a new model for business is sorely needed, the authors probe the dominant paradigm of individualism and shareholder maximization that has dominated American business over the past thirty years. This critical and timely book offers a challenge to global business leaders and all thoughtful citizens who wish to understand the path forward for business."

—Rakesh Khurana, Marvin Bower Professor of Leadership Development, Harvard Business School

"In a fast transforming world, leadership can be a source of purpose and inspiration or can become a source of inertia. In this wonderful book we discover the role leaders can play to steer their companies with purpose, compassion, and authenticity. Deep insights, fresh thinking, and creative actions make this a must read for every future-oriented leader."

—Lynda Gratton, Professor of Management Practice, London Business School; author, *The Shift: The Future of Work Is Already Here*

"*Higher Ambition* expertly details the stories of leaders who connect the dots between economic performance and social value. Building strategic purpose, organizational integrity, and stakeholder relationships are challenging tasks for leaders today. This book offers pragmatic lessons for success, drawn from leaders who have been there."

—Dominic Barton, Global Managing Director, McKinsey & Company

"Why do companies with higher ambitions achieve better financial success than those with narrower goals? And given that they do succeed, why don't more companies follow a more ambitious path? *Higher Ambition* provides the first comprehensive set of answers to those timeless and important questions. The authors show how higher ambition is vital to long-term success, and they demonstrate what sorts of leadership skills are needed to make it meaningful to the full range of stakeholders in the company. This book will provide inspiration and practical advice to any executive who wants their company to become a force for good in society."

—Julian Birkinshaw, Professor of Strategy &
Entrepreneurship, London Business School

"I think that it is a superb book—a real game-changer. The authors have gone well beyond existing theory in rounding out a superior leadership model."

—Paul Lawrence, Wallace Brett Donham Professor of Organizational
Behavior, Emeritus, Harvard Business School

"*Higher Ambition* addresses a critically important topic, made even more pressing by recent events. The authors provide a new framework for business. What they stress— as I have also discovered—is when leaders focus on optimizing a higher purpose and economic value, they get more of both."

—Richard W. Gochnauer, CEO, United Stationers Inc.

HIGHER
AMBITION

HIGHER AMBITION
HOW GREAT LEADERS CREATE ECONOMIC *and* SOCIAL VALUE

MICHAEL BEER / RUSSELL EISENSTAT
NATHANIEL FOOTE / TOBIAS FREDBERG
FLEMMING NORRGREN

HARVARD BUSINESS REVIEW PRESS / BOSTON, MASSACHUSETTS

Library of Congress Cataloging-in-Publication Data

Higher ambition : how great leaders create economic and social value /
Michael Beer . . . [et al.].
    p. cm.
  Includes bibliographical references.
  ISBN 978-1-4221-5974-3 (alk. paper)
  1. Leadership.   2. Strategic planning.   3. Social responsibility of business.
4. Success in business.   I. Beer, Michael.
  HD57.7.H533 2011
  658.4'092—dc22

                                            2011007466

Contents

Introduction

O VER THE LAST FOUR YEARS, we have engaged with, learned from, and been inspired by thirty-six CEOs from around the world, all of whom share a higher ambition. These leaders are not content to just make their quarterly numbers; they are committed to creating institutions that sustainably win, with their people, their customers, their communities, *and* with their shareholders. These leaders are working to fully realize the potential of their firms to create superior and lasting economic value. At the same time, they are putting their shoulders to the wheel to create superior social value. And they seek to accomplish both goals *simultaneously*.

That is their higher ambition.

This ambition distinguishes the companies we profile in this book from those that focus primarily on building financial wealth and only secondarily pay attention to the social nature of their organizations. It also sets these companies apart from those that equate social value solely with corporate philanthropy or think of it as just giving back to the community; although these are worthy pursuits, they do not in and of themselves lead to the creation of a lasting and valuable social institution.

For each of the CEOs we include in this book, higher ambition— although defined with some individual distinctions—is similarly understood.

By superior *economic* value, these leaders typically mean that the company consistently meets or exceeds short-term performance expectations, outperforms its industry peers for a meaningful period of years, and does both in a way that contributes to long-term advantage. By superior *social* value, our leaders mean that they are building lasting institutions that both contribute to the social good (building a better world) and create social capital (relationships with employees, customers, communities, and others characterized by distinctive levels of trust and mutual commitment). Higher-ambition leaders understand that these two dimensions of social value are mutually reinforcing. Contributing to the social good builds trust and commitment, while this commitment in turn is reinforced by the sense of meaning created by contributing to building a better world.

We should also make clear that, for the CEOs of these companies, higher ambition does not pertain to personal gain. These leaders are, of course, ambitious and successful people who push themselves hard and achieve a great deal, but their ambition is distinctly *not* about maximizing organizational power or being the highest paid CEO.

The higher-ambition CEOs we interviewed operated in a wide variety of industries across three continents. They led private companies, public companies, nonprofits, and hybrids; some were very large, some relatively small; some had existed for over a century, others were start-ups. Some of the leaders had been at their posts for extended periods of time; others had served more briefly. They came from a variety of cultures, had varying educational and professional backgrounds, and lived very different kinds of lives.

They had, however, certain important characteristics in common. None claimed to be superstars or models of management perfection. They spoke to us with candor, insight, detail, and a degree of humility about themselves, their companies, and what they do and don't do. Many told us to highlight the collective contributions of the team around them more than their own.

They revealed themselves to be thoughtful practitioners of the craft of leadership, whose insights, taken together, define an approach to leadership that is distinctive and substantially different from mainstream practice. They all were uncompromising in their commitment to simultaneously create both economic and social value; neither financial gain nor social worth alone was a sufficient outcome for any of them.

Our research method was quite simple. We decided to work from the "leaders out" rather than from the "scholar or consultant in." That is, beyond the idea that today's exemplary company is the one that creates both economic and social value, we did not set out to prove a hypothesis about how such value is actually achieved. Rather, we chose to listen carefully, observe closely, then analyze the material, and, finally, synthesize what we had learned.

We did not intend this study to test a hypothesis nor did we set out to show that companies that outperform their peers do so because of their values or people-centric cultures. There are a number of studies that have already shown that relationship.[1] Rather, we were interested in learning about an area that is far less well understood: the critical roles and practices of leadership that contribute to creating superior and sustained economic and social value. We sought leaders across a wide range of industries and geographies with sufficient commitment, experience, capability, and self-awareness that they had something genuine and important to say on this topic.

We make no claims that the leaders we spoke with are the "best" CEOs, rigorously chosen from a comprehensive scientific sample, or that any of these CEOs are without their faults. (In fact, one of the defining characteristics of these leaders was a greater awareness of their limitations than some of their peers typically have.) This is what our more academic colleagues would call an exploratory or hypothesis-generating study. What we were after was not scientific proof but practical insights from CEOs with something genuine and thoughtful to say. (See table I-1 for a list of the

TABLE I-1

Leaders and companies in the sample

Leader	Organization	Country
Anu Aga	Thermax, Ltd.	India
Torben Ballegaard Sørensen	Bang & Olufsen Group	Denmark
Carl Bennet	Getinge Group	Sweden
Paul Bulcke	Nestlé	Switzerland
Christian Clausen	Nordea	Sweden
Bertrand Collomb	Lafarge	France
Douglas R. Conant	Campbell Soup Company	United States
Anders Dahlvig	IKEA	Netherlands/Sweden
Roger Dickhout	Pineridge Group	Canada
Peter Dunn	Steak 'n Shake	United States
Russell Fradin	Aon Hewitt	United States
Kenneth W. Freeman	Quest Diagnostics	United States
William W. George	Medtronic	United States
Val Gooding	BUPA	Great Britain
Steven H. Holtzman	Infinity Pharmaceuticals	United States
Sherrill W. Hudson	TECO Energy	United States
Leif Johansson	Volvo Group	Sweden
Gary C. Kelly	Southwest Airlines	United States
David H. Langstaff	Veridian Corporation	United States
Allan Leighton	Royal Mail	Great Britain
David H. Lissy	Bright Horizons	United States
Edward J. Ludwig	Becton, Dickinson & Co.	United States
Anand G. Mahindra	Mahindra & Mahindra	India
Dale F. Morrison	McCain Foods Ltd.	Canada
N. R. Narayana Murthy	Infosys	India

Leader	Organization	Country
Archie Norman	Asda	Great Britain
Jorma Ollila	Nokia	Finland
Stefan Persson	H&M	Sweden
Carlo Pesenti	Italcementi Group	Italy
Dick Pettingill	Allina Hospitals & Clinics	United States
Peter Sands	Standard Chartered Bank	Great Britain
Marjorie Scardino	Pearson	Great Britain
Tim Solso	Cummins Inc.	United States
Douglas W. Stotlar	Con-Way Inc.	United States
Ratan N. Tata	Tata Group	India
Brian C. Walker	Herman Miller	United States

leaders and companies in the sample. Also see the appendix for more details on our research methodology.)

To find these CEOs, we relied on recommendations from trusted colleagues, our own direct experience in working with some of these leaders, as well as the usual lists of most admired companies and best places to work. As a check on our judgment and to keep ourselves honest, we applied two tests:

1. Their company had to have had a compounded annual growth rate in revenues, profits, and market capitalization that exceeded the fiftieth percentile of industry peers between 1997 and 2006, or for the CEO tenure. We used corresponding figures for public or privately held organizations.

2. The CEOs were concerned with developing a people-centric, high-commitment culture, based on evidence from the public record—articles, speeches, and views of those with direct knowledge.

The CEOs we profile here are not the first to have built and led businesses that achieved superior financial results and were also seen as valuable social enterprises, nor is this the first book to have documented such companies. Our higher-ambition CEOs have read and admired such works as *In Search of Excellence, Built to Last*, and *Good to Great*, and were proud to think of themselves as following in the tradition of the companies profiled in them. Michael Porter and Rosabeth Moss Kanter have also written about the symbiotic relationship between social and economic value.[2] We also see the themes identified in this book as quite consistent with those we have found in our own previous work, including most recently, Mike Beer's book, *High Commitment, High Performance*.[3] There are, however, two important differences of note, first about the current business context and, second, about this book.

Higher-ambition CEOs are operating in a complex, pressurized global business environment that encompasses a greater diversity in national cultures, ethnicity, gender, and religion than ever before. In addition, they have had to build and sustain their companies in the context of an extremely well-developed market for corporate control, where the survival of the CEO—and the company itself—can depend on meeting quarterly earnings goals. This later factor, along with the truly extraordinary rewards that the CEO who pushes for glittering short-term financial results can reap, has helped to create the massive crisis in corporate legitimacy that we see unfolding around the world. That crisis is likely one of the reasons that the higher-ambition CEOs agreed to talk with us. They wanted to tell their stories and to differentiate themselves from those corporate executives who were grabbing the headlines, often in less-than-admirable ways. They wanted to distinguish their strong, grounded companies from those constructed on shaky foundations.

As for this book, our goal goes beyond the descriptive to the prescriptive. The CEOs that we describe here have been converging on a distinctive way to lead and manage that they, and we, believe delivers better and more sustainable results in both economic and social terms. Indeed, their simultaneous pursuit of these dual objectives, we assert, is precisely why they are able to succeed. As we will describe, by focusing on the social dimension, they are able to create an organizational model that is both higher energy and lower friction, which allows them to succeed in economic terms. In turn, by succeeding in creating economic value, they are able to invest over time in ways that deliver superior outcomes to their key stakeholders and society as well as sustain the institution's social fabric. As one higher-ambition CEO, Peter Dunn, explained to us, "Creating social value unlocks the dormant creative energies that exist in all of us, which in turn creates outstanding financial results. Conversely, with growing profits, you are able to attract and energize people over time. Creating both social and economic value directly reinforces the primary motivators of people: purpose, autonomy, and mastery."

Yet, if leading to create both economic and social value is so powerful, why do so few current CEOs pursue this path? We believe this is not primarily due to lack of good intent, but because productively managing the tension between financial results and social value is far from easy. It requires a CEO to make tough business decisions such as restructuring or outsourcing—which may be necessary for a firm's financial viability—in ways that don't compromise an institution's core human values and integrity. It requires the CEO personally to move out of the protective cocoon created by support staff, advisers, and counselors, and corporate jets and comfortable perks to confront the truth about the firm's (and their own) strengths and weaknesses.

To take on such work is tough enough. But CEOs have, in our opinion, been less inclined to do so because they don't have enough models to emulate, nor is there a rich literature that sets out lessons and describes in detail the methods, practices, and tools that higher-ambition leaders can use to achieve their goals. *It is this urgent need for grounded and specific leadership methods and behaviors to which we have responded with this book.*

Our focus here is to go beyond a discussion of the general nature of higher-ambition leadership and provide a compendium of the practical. Collectively, these leaders are pointing the way to a distinctive leadership model that we illustrate through their individual practices. Exactly *what* do our leaders do? *How* do they go about their tasks and fulfill their responsibilities? Of course, not all of these leaders exhibit all elements of the model: what we are offering is an integrated picture, synthesized from their individual examples.

Our hope is that our approach—which seeks to deliver deep understanding along with useful advice, all originating with leaders who have been there and done that—will provide readers with new insight, new inspiration, and new courage in shouldering their own work of leadership and in pursuing and achieving their own higher ambition.

A Guide to the Contents of the Book

We cannot reduce higher-ambition leadership to a simple checklist of key success factors or to a two-by-two table of leadership attributes; the whole goes well beyond the sum of the parts. With this in mind, in part I, "Higher-Ambition Leadership in Action," we provide an integrated view of higher-ambition leadership.

- In chapter 1, "Leading with a Higher Ambition," we provide a picture of the kind of leadership needed to achieve a higher ambition, focusing on Doug Conant and how he "put the chicken back in the chicken noodle soup" at Campbell Soup Company. We add several other examples, including Narayana Murthy of Infosys.

- In chapter 2, "The Simultaneous Solve," we focus on the story of CEO Peter Sands and the transformation of Standard Chartered Bank from a second-tier global player into an international insider to illustrate how he and other higher-ambition leaders achieve a "simultaneous solve" that creates both economic and social value.

In part II, "The Disciplines of Higher-Ambition Leadership," we highlight the distinctive approach that higher-ambition leaders take to the core disciplines of general management. At the end of each chapter in this part, we provide a summary table that shows how higher-ambition leaders both embrace and go significantly beyond traditional management "best practices."

- In chapter 3, "Forging Strategic Identity," we show how strategy development in higher-ambition companies goes well beyond an analytic and numbers-driven exercise and becomes a fundamental rethinking of a firm's *strategic identity*, as we illustrate through the story of Nokia, its CEO Jorma Ollila, and the company's development of the cell phone.

- In chapter 4, "Building a Shared Commitment to Excel," we describe how performance management, which typically is centered on negotiation about financial targets, becomes, in higher-ambition companies, a shared commitment to deliver a dramatically higher level of value not just to shareholders, but also to customers, communities, and employees. At Mahindra & Mahindra, CEO Anand Mahindra helped the company dramatically improve its ability to perform by internalizing a new set of execution disciplines and capabilities.

- In chapter 5, "Creating Community out of Diversity," through the stories of Cummins and CEO Tim Solso and several others, we'll see how companies reinvent, despite increasing diversity and global scale, the sense of shared purpose and community that provide the emotional core and binding energy to accomplish ambitious goals that might otherwise be unattainable.

- In chapter 6, "Leading with *Sisu,*" we explore the stories of Leif Johansson at Volvo and others, and show how achieving a higher ambition requires personal leadership that engages, sustains trust, and provides clear, consistent direction, as well as a dogged, determined commitment that is best captured by the Finnish word, *sisu,* which essentially means "guts."

- In chapter 7, "Committing to Collective Leadership," we highlight the powerful role of the broader leadership team in achieving success, and the inordinate level of energy and creativity these CEOs commit to building and aligning collective leadership at multiple levels, through the stories of Val Gooding at BUPA and others.

In part III, "Moving to a Higher Ambition," we take a step back and consider the broader implications of what we have learned about how leaders, companies, and business as a whole can more rapidly and powerfully achieve their higher ambitions.

- In chapter 8, "Becoming a Higher-Ambition Leader," we share the key lessons we have learned about how leaders can develop their own abilities to lead with higher ambition.

- In chapter 9, "A Higher Ambition for Business," we offer some final thoughts on the meaning and importance of higher-ambition leadership and its implications for the role of boards, business schools, and the broader institutional context.

The reader can find additional supporting materials on higher-ambition leadership at www.higherambition.com.

Part One

Higher-Ambition Leadership in Action

1

Leading with a Higher Ambition

It's believing in the potential of what you want to be, as opposed to describing what you are. That intention ... attracts opportunities to you.

—Roger Dickhout, cofounder and
CEO of Pineridge Group

WHAT DOES IT TAKE to lead with a higher ambition? What are the core characteristics and capabilities of the leader who is able to build and sustain institutions that create both economic and social value? How does he or she approach the task of leadership?

Consider Doug Conant, CEO of Campbell Soup Company.

Russ Eisenstat and a colleague, Chris Richmond, met with Conant at his office in Camden, New Jersey, to discuss how, under his leadership, Campbell had returned from a near-death experience to its current position as one of the world's most successful food companies. For Conant, a highly regarded executive with nearly thirty-five years in the food industry, the Campbell story is about strategy and performance, leadership and organization, but he never forgets that it is just as fundamentally about food and nutrition. So it was perhaps not surprising that we started with a brief discussion of his diet.

Conant stands 6'1" and carries himself like the relative of a president of Harvard, which he is. He had sprained an ankle not long before our meeting, which meant he had not been able to follow his normal workout routine and had put on a few pounds that he wanted to shed. So his lunch consisted of a Campbell's microwavable Soup at Hand cup followed by a banana. Somebody had suggested to Conant that he call it the soup-and-fruit diet. He replied, "I said, no, my diet is Soup at Hand and a banana. That's more memorable. And, as my wife says, it's something so easy even a CEO can do it. I can use the microwave and I know how to peel a banana."

A well-developed sense of humor and a willingness to poke fun at himself in this way characterized our interview with Conant. Many of the other CEOs we talked with were equally self-deprecating. Leif Johansson, CEO of Volvo, told us, for example, that being CEO "may affect you with a personality disorder by making you think you know everything. But you don't actually." Johansson is especially wary of this troubling syndrome because Volvo is "an institution in Swedish society," and as a result, "when you have become the big boss, they all think: 'If he'll just say something, it's so very relevant.' But it's by no means certain that it is."

Johansson and Conant and the other leaders we profile in this book are refreshingly aware of the "big boss" problem, and while they understand their responsibilities and the significant influence they have on people's lives and livelihoods, they are fundamentally healthy people.

As we'll discuss in this chapter, these leaders:

- See the glass whole.

- Envision the potential.

- Set worthy goals.

- Don't compromise on the things that matter.

See the Glass Whole

Some of those we interviewed were lucky enough to lead companies like H&M, IKEA, Nestlé, and Southwest Airlines that had, for decades, been high-performing enterprises that had also been creating social value. In those companies, CEOs rose from the inside, were products of the system, and could take proactive measures to renew business health and avoid getting into trouble. However, not all of our leaders were so lucky.

When Conant became CEO of Campbell Soup in January 2001, he walked into a once-great company that was in steep decline. A consultancy informed Jorma Ollila, CEO of Nokia, in 1991 that his company was not "supposed to survive." Anand Mahindra, CEO of Mahindra & Mahindra, took over during a crisis that engulfed both the company and its home country, India. Mahindra & Mahindra made its first operating loss ever, Mahindra recalled, at the same time that the Indian economy crashed: "Because of that crisis, India opened up and liberalized." As a result, Mahindra & Mahindra, which had grown as a monopoly, suddenly had to compete in the world marketplace.

Val Gooding, CEO of the British health-care company BUPA, told us that she only realized after she joined that the organization "was in quite such a mess." As she put it, "The core business wasn't making any money. The customer service was poor. In my first few weeks, three or four of the senior managers came in and said, 'Oh, we're glad you've come, because this will need sorting out. And oh, by the way, if you can't sort it out, we're all leaving.'"

So Conant was hardly the only one of the executives we interviewed to be dropped into a corporate landscape that had undergone great disruption.

"From 1990 to 1996, Campbell Soup Company was one of the best-performing food companies in the world," Conant told us. "Sales grew nicely. Margins went as high as 24 percent. The company had strong share, particularly in the U.S. soup market where there was little direct competition." Then, caught up in the market's obsession with short-term profits, but unable to substantially build its mature business by increasing sales volume, Campbell decided that its best choice was to leverage its strong U.S. market position to raise prices and achieve the profit growth that its stakeholders had come to expect. It kept raising prices until other companies, like Progresso and several private-label brands, saw an opportunity to compete more aggressively in the U.S. market where Campbell had been operating virtually unchallenged. The new brands appeared on shelves at prices sufficiently lower than those of comparable Campbell's soups to cause consumers to consider switching. Soon the newcomers gained market share, at Campbell's expense.

The company either could not see what was happening to it or was unable to come up with a strategy to fight back. "So essentially, they said, 'Well, we can't take any more on price, so we'll have to lean on productivity,'" Conant explained. "And that's when they started to do things like taking the chicken out of the chicken noodle soup."

To Conant, this was a significant turning point: Campbell was actually starting to compromise on the quality of its chicken noodle soup recipe, the product it had launched in 1934 and that had become an iconic American food. Now this staple of the national pantry, and of the company's product portfolio, was starting to be stripped of its most important asset, chicken.

"That's when the organization entered 'the circle of doom,'" Conant said. Prices could not be raised any higher, because that would certainly lead to a further erosion of market share. Additional gains in productivity were unrealistic. The only easy line item left to cut was the marketing budget, which they began to do. But advertising had been "propping up the brand," as Conant put it, and when there was less of it, sales dropped even more. "Then they had no more consumer spending to cut and the business wasn't improving," Conant said. "So they began to fire people. Two hundred people from R&D in one day. And then there was nobody to do the work. So the whole thing just came crashing down."

From 1997 to 2001, Campbell went from being one of the highest-performing food companies in the world to being one of the worst; the share price dropped from $60 to $30. That's when the board recruited Conant, an industry veteran who had worked for three of the world's leading food companies—General Mills, Inc.; Kraft Foods; and the Nabisco Foods Company, where he had achieved five consecutive years of double-digit earnings growth.

"They gave me carte blanche to look under all the rocks," Conant said, "and challenged me to come back with a candid assessment of the situation. They weren't looking for a quick fix. They were looking to become a sustainable, good company."

The ability to look carefully at one's company and see what is actually there—positive, negative, simple, complex, known, unknown—is an important characteristic of all our leaders. This is not about optimism or pessimism, seeing the glass as half-full or half-empty, but about being able to step back and see the whole glass, the entire company as it is and has been.

Envision the Potential

Another characteristic that sets our leaders apart balances that ability to see the reality of a company: the ability to envision and believe in a company's potential and to understand, within an environment often characterized by confusion, crisis, and underperformance, the real possibilities for success. The combination is essential. On the one hand, these executives see the reality with clarity. This keeps them from being easily deluded or distracted, builds the confidence and trust of those around them that they "get it," and motivates them to make difficult decisions about which activities to pursue and which to jettison, as well as which people to retain and which to encourage into other endeavors. But they also see the potential with real excitement and enthusiasm. As Roger Dickhout, cofounder and CEO of Pineridge Group, put it: "It's believing in the potential of what you want to be, as opposed to describing what you are. That intention attracts opportunities to you."

The ability to envision a company's potential—a kind of informed faith, a hardheaded optimism—is one of the defining characteristics of the CEOs in our study. Why else would an experienced and thoughtful executive like Conant want to join a company like Campbell when it was in such distress? What made Conant think he could transform Campbell? What did he see that others did not? What intrigued and attracted him to the challenge?

The short answer is that he did his homework. Before taking over as CEO of Campbell, Conant thought deeply about how this legendary company, founded in 1860, had gotten trapped in a circle of doom, and he came to some unique insights. "They were under pressure from all sides," Conant said. There was, at the time, an axiomatic belief in the consumer packaged goods industry that scale always brought benefits, such as the muscle needed for wide distribution and the volume required to keep prices low. Accordingly, starting in the 1980s, the U.S. industry began a period of consolidation: Kraft bought Nabisco, Unilever bought Best Foods, Kellogg bought Keebler, and General Mills bought Pillsbury.

This belief in the importance of scale came about at least partly because of the remarkable rise of Walmart, which, with its almost unimaginable scale and relentless focus on everyday low prices, was rapidly attaining the position it holds today as the largest and most powerful food retailer in the United States. Even as industry suppliers began to merge and combine, so too did the main players in the food retailing industry, Campbell's customers. As another way to compete with Walmart and other big-box stores, the food suppliers and their retail partners stepped up their development of private-label products. And just to add to the turmoil in the food industry, consumers were getting harder and harder to connect with, largely because they had so many buying options available to them and because marketing and consumer communications had grown much more complex than ever before.

"So," Conant said, "you had the consumers, the competition, the customers, and the suppliers all putting pressure on the portfolio. And the question was, 'How is Campbell going to survive?'"

Certainly not by raising prices, cutting key ingredients, reducing marketing expenditure, or gutting the company of talent. During that period of due diligence, Conant and his team studied other players in the industry and came to a rather surprising conclusion: scale was not as important as it appeared. "We looked at the companies that had created the most value over the last thirty years and found that they were not the large diversified food companies with broad portfolios," Conant said. "The names were Wrigley, Hershey, and McCormick. These companies had powerful number-one brands, were in categories that had the wind at their back, and had the financial wherewithal to support the brands. They were also companies where there was a strong, dedicated organization, where everybody knew what was expected, and there was a performance ethic."

In other words, they were companies quite like the one that Campbell had previously been; they had not merged their way to greatness and they did not rely on massive scale to create exceptional value. They did it through category focus, key brands, and, significantly, through strong organizations. Armed with these insights, Conant became convinced of Campbell's potential, despite the current discouraging picture on virtually all fronts.

In October 2000, while still one of several candidates for the job, Conant met with six members of the board of directors. He provided his analysis of the situation, followed by the framework of a revitalization plan. His key message was that the situation was "broken, but fixable." What's more, he said, "The situation is deteriorating rapidly. It demands swift, decisive action." Conant finished off by revealing his optimistic side: he told the directors that he was "enthusiastic about the challenge" and could quickly put a superb team in place that could help him meet it.

In January, the company offered Conant the position of CEO, and he accepted. In late February, he had his first chance to share his view of the company's potential at an industry conference organized by the Consumer Analyst Group of New York (CAGNY), a three-day meeting of analysts who convene each year in New York to hear presentations by executives from food, beverage, tobacco, and household/personal products companies. At that meeting, an analyst asked Conant what his plans were. He said, "I've only been here six weeks, but we have to grow this business." How would he go about doing that? Conant's answer was the most fundamental and, as a result, the most shocking one he could give. He said, "We will grow condensed soup."

This caused quite a reaction. Everyone knew that condensed soup was Campbell's signature product, that it had been in decline for twenty-five years, and that "everybody and their brother had tried to rejuvenate it," as Conant put it. Its reputation as a mediocre product, out of step with the times, seemed irremediable. But Conant believed the potential lay in condensed soup, and that's what he said in public. "I had to declare something that was bold," Conant said. "And I had to believe it, because I was dead if we didn't."

The analysts scoffed. Wrote Louis Lavelle in *Business Week*:

Conant needs to begin the long, hard task of fundamentally remaking the company. Slow-growing for years, Campbell has resisted change and missed opportunities. Its slavish devotion to condensed soup left faster-growing products lacking for research-and-development funds and marketing support. Without a major makeover, the core product appears destined for irrelevance. Says Prudential Securities analyst John M. McMillan: "You really have to ask yourself: 'Is this the next buggy whip?'"[1]

Reed Abelson, writing in the *New York Times,* also quoted McMillan, one of the industry's best-known analysts. "And, clearly, consumer tastes have changed. 'They basically have the Maxwell House of soup,' said John McMillan, an analyst at Prudential Securities, referring to the once-dominant brand of coffee that fell victim to changing preferences and chains like Starbucks that spare consumers the bother of brewing their own."[2]

Conant remembers the remarks vividly. "McMillan called our company, and our soup business, a buggy whip," Conant said. "He said the soup was introduced in 1869, and it's the same damned can of soup it was then. Now you're going to turn that around? Well, good luck!"

Conant understood the objections, but refused to be swayed by them. "You've got to have fierce resolve to drive through and take the organization to higher ground," he said. "The challenge was declaring myself, not quite knowing how we were going do it, then moving forward with determination. You have board members asking, 'How are you going to grow condensed soup? Shouldn't we just get out of the soup business and do something else? Shouldn't we just stop playing around in the U.S. and go global?' You're getting hell from everybody. So, I just had to systematically go about putting in place the things necessary to grow the business when all the people working on it were doubtful. And 'doubtful' is putting it kindly."

For Conant, the challenge was to see that, even in a product as familiar as condensed soup and a company that was more than a century old, there was still enormous potential for improved performance and even growth.

Set Worthy Goals

Early in his tenure, Conant articulated some worthy goals for Campbell Soup that were very different from those most CEOs taking charge of a troubled company would set. He introduced a paradigm that he called the "Campbell Success Model." It had two main components, one financial and one social. "We needed to outperform our peer companies in the marketplace," he told us. "We called that, 'winning in the marketplace.' And along with that—and this is the thing that had been so horribly neglected— we had to create a superior employment experience for each and every employee, relative to their other employment options. We called that 'winning in the workplace.' We said, 'We have to win on both fronts.' If you're not winning in the workplace, you can't win the marketplace in a sustainable way and be sustainably good company. Our goal was to increase the value of the enterprise." Later, Conant and his top team added "contributing to the community."

In other words, Conant declared that Campbell would henceforth be concerned with both financial success and social value, with both short-term results and long-term sustainability. There would be no more compromises on either dimension.

Dick Pettingill, who turned around Allina Hospitals & Clinics in Minneapolis, Minnesota, and made it a model of a high-performing health-care system, told us that his sense of purpose and his values were central to his identity and ambition for that organization: "It's grounded in purpose. It's grounded in values. It's grounded in mission. And, at the end of the day, when I leave here, I hope I have made a significant difference in people's lives in the state of Minnesota. It's not more complicated than that. I counsel people that it's not about the competition; it's about making a difference in people's lives. So I'm constantly taking people back to a sense of greater purpose, of the nobility of what we're doing. If we can change the health care in that backyard, when you go out the front door here, then we have something to give back to the transformation of health care in America today."

No story conveys how these leaders connect personal values to firm goals and how they integrate business goals with the interests of multiple constituents better than that of Narayana Murthy and India's Infosys. In 1981, with $250 in capital that his wife had saved from her teaching job, Murthy and a small team founded Infosys. As Murthy explained to our colleague Malcolm

Wolf, he and his team saw the main opportunity as "liberating the power of Indian engineering talent" to meet the burgeoning demand for large, customized software solutions, focusing first on the U.S. market, where the demand was greatest, and then expanding around the world. But Murthy also believed that, to realize the greatest potential, they would have to think about the nature and intent of the company in a new way.

Infosys got started, as so many technology companies seem to, in the founder's apartment. Murthy and his management team got together "to discover what the objectives of the company should be." At first, the objectives suggested were the rather obvious ones, all based on the creation of financial value. "One said we should become the largest software company in India in revenues," Murthy recalled. "Somebody else said we should be the most profitable software company. A third person said we should be the company with the highest market capitalization in our industry." At the end of this discussion, Murthy proposed a different objective: "I suggested to my colleagues to consider becoming the most respected company in India. Not just in our industry, but amongst all the companies in India."

Murthy, in other words, expressed a higher ambition for his company from the very start. Yes, it should succeed by all the standard financial measures, but it should also set its sights on becoming an institution with a different and additional kind of worth.

Murthy explained to us why he believed that respect was so important:

> If you want respect, then you have to do the right things. And doing the right things is entirely under your control—being honest, being ethical, being respectful of others, keeping up the dignity of other people. If you seek respect from customers, you will not shortchange them. You will satisfy them in an honest and ethical way. If you seek respect from fellow employees, you'll be open with them, you'll be honest with them, you'll be fair with them, you will keep up their dignity. If you seek respect from investors, then you follow the finest

principles of corporate governance, and you will operate as trustees on their behalf. If you seek respect from your vendor partners, you will be sympathetic to them, and you will come to their aid in the hour of their need, so that they will come to your need when you are in trouble. And if you seek respect from the government of the land, wherever you operate, then you will never violate any law of the land. And finally, if you seek respect from the society, wherever you operate, whether India, U.S., the U.K., or China, wherever it is, you will conduct yourself in a manner that enhances the goodwill for you from the society.

After presenting his reasoning about the value of respect, Murthy expressed a view common to our CEOs: "I said, if you did all of these things, revenues will automatically come. Profits will automatically come. And consequently, market capital additionally will come."

That is exactly what happened. Infosys created significant financial value. From 1981 to 2010, it grew from a market capitalization of $250 million to $38 billion. And the company also gained enormous respect. Since 2000, Infosys has been voted the "Most Admired Indian Company" in the *Wall Street Journal Asia 200* for ten years in a row, showing how developing a higher-ambition aspiration and vision at the start creates economic value, not just social value.

As Murthy summed it up, "I'm glad that my colleagues accepted my argument."

Don't Compromise on the Things That Matter

We describe Conant, Johansson, and the other leaders profiled in this book as *uncompromising*. This was the word we used in our 2008 article in *Harvard Business Review* to describe the CEOs in our research.[3] As our thinking progressed, we left the word behind for a while, largely because we worried that it might bring to mind traits associated with one or more of those CEO stereotypes that we're trying to avoid: "rigidity," "inflexibility," "focus on the self."

But, as we explored further, we returned to the word *uncompromising* as the best and most distinctive way to describe the essential nature of the CEOs we had come to know so well. It is not that they are inflexible or rigid in their thinking—quite the contrary. But these leaders will not bend when it comes to vital issues that they deeply believe have an important impact on the company's ability to create social or financial value.

The ability of our CEOs to stick to their guns applies not only to their company's efforts but to their personal conduct as well. "I start out with what's important to me," Conant said. "And it's a lot more than work. My work is important, but my family is important. My community is important. I'm involved in my church and my own personal well-being." Conant pointed out a plaque that was hanging on the wall behind him. "That's my personal mission statement," he said. "It says that these are the five things that are important to me. This is why I'm on this earth. Every month or so, I look at that mission statement. I ask, 'Am I hitting on all five cylinders?' Now, am I going to go high on them every day? No. Every week? No. But if I can't look at the list and say, 'I'm attending to these five things, I'm living a well-rounded life,' experience says that I won't be operating at peak performance for very long. I'm relentless about it. I make sure there's family time. I make sure there's personal time. You've got to either take control of it or it takes control of you."

As we said earlier, we do not assert that Conant and Murthy and the other CEOs we spoke with are superheroes, but that does not mean that they are in any way ordinary. They are smart, educated, and successful. They operate with integrity and a disciplined focus. They expect a great deal of themselves, as well as of others, and are capable of personally performing at a high level over long periods of time and through challenging episodes.

Uncompromising leaders combine immodest ambitions and modest behavior, or, as Conant put it, they are "tough on standards, but tender with people." Conant said that if we were to survey his leadership team, "you'd probably find they think I'm a marshmallow."

Conclusion

While envisioning the potential of their companies and setting worthy goals, the higher-ambition CEOs did not know the precise road map to get there. Conant did not know how Campbell would grow the condensed soup business. Murthy did not know how Infosys was going to become the most respected company in India. But they were committing themselves and their companies to a process of mobilization, learning, and discovery that progressively unlocked more of the company's full potential.

What is involved, as we will see later in this book, is a flexible and iterative approach to the core disciplines of developing strategy, managing performance, building a strong culture, and developing leadership capability.

In this work, these leaders are guided by a strong sense of *integrity*. By integrity, we mean something that includes, but goes beyond, honesty and ethics. Certainly, our leaders work as hard as is humanly possible to integrate their decisions and actions with their values and beliefs. But they also are skilled at *integrating* actions in different domains of the business, ranging from strategy and finance to people management. They see actions in domains that are usually considered separately as being connected and mutually reinforcing. In the next chapter, we will describe more fully the "simultaneous solve" they achieve across these dimensions.

And higher-ambition CEOs are more likely than others to see things *whole*—to sense both the challenges and potential before them. It is perhaps this willingness to see their companies and themselves in full, with all their diversity and complexity, that contributes to our CEOs' ability to achieve their higher ambition for the creation of both financial and social value.

Certainly, for Conant and Campbell Soup Company, it has paid off. In the company's 2009 annual report, Conant wrote, "I am pleased to report that our five-year cumulative total share-owner return, including stock price appreciation and dividends, was twice that of the S&P Packaged Foods Index, at 37.3 percent versus 18.2 percent, even though our return for the rolling three-year period ending in fiscal 2009 fell modestly below the peer index." In addition, Campbell reported world-class levels of employee engagement and was named to *Corporate Responsibility* magazine's 100 Best Corporate Citizens list.

And condensed soup sales—the stodgy old product that Conant swore to revive—grew by 5 percent in 2009. The talk of buggy whips and Maxwell House coffee has faded away. Readers will also be pleased to know that chicken has been fully restored to Campbell's chicken noodle soup.

2

The Simultaneous Solve

*Fundamentally, what drives me is to shape the
organization simultaneously to be very effective
in terms of performance, a great place to work,
and something that is actually a force for good.*

—Peter Sands, Standard Chartered Bank

OR HIGHER-AMBITION CEOS, the work of economic and
social value creation involves a set of core management disciplines—developing strategy, managing performance, building a
shared culture, and personally leading their people—but the CEOs do not
approach the tasks associated with these disciplines sequentially or in isolation. Rather, they practice these disciplines in a mutually reinforcing way
to achieve a "simultaneous solve." That is, they develop and execute against
an integrated agenda that allows them to deliver superior economic and
social value simultaneously.

Peter Sands, CEO of Standard Chartered Bank (SCB), told us about a
rather unusual and especially telling example of the simultaneous solve in
action. One morning in the fall of 2006, Sands, who had recently been appointed CEO of SCB, stepped on stage to address the annual gathering of
the bank's top four hundred executives. As he settled behind the podium,

he looked out over his audience. Although the men and women represented all the geographic areas where SCB does business, the majority of them hailed from countries in Asia, Africa, and the Middle East.

Sands, a former McKinsey & Company director, had joined the bank in 2002 as chief financial officer and, not surprisingly, was primarily known as a numbers guy. But, instead of launching into a discussion of performance results and financial targets, as his audience might have expected, Sands flashed up on the screen a picture of a young girl and a young boy on a swing in Singapore. "I think this girl was my first girlfriend," he said and paused. The audience cocked its collective head. What was he up to? Where was the data? Who was this person? "The picture was taken when I was two years old," Sands said, after a moment. "My family lived in Singapore, and the girl on the left in the photo was my nanny's daughter."

Sands's surprising introduction made a lasting impression on his audience. "I dithered a long time before doing it, because this is not stuff that I'm comfortable talking about," Sands told Nathaniel Foote and Tobias Fredberg during a conversation in SCB's London offices. But Sands was trying to make a very specific point about himself and the bank with this gesture. Just as SCB has a much stronger presence in Asia than it does in the West, and just as the majority of the senior executives in the audience were from Asian countries, Sands, too, thinks of himself as having Asian roots. Both his parents were born in Southeast Asia, and Sands, spent much of his boyhood there, looked after by the Malay nanny whose daughter was in the picture he had shown to his audience of managers. His intention, therefore, was not only to reveal a bit about his background, but to reveal very specifically how his personal identity and the bank's identity had similar resonances.

"I'm very, very glad I did that," Sands told us when we first met with him, in April 2007, just six months into his new role as CEO. He continued, "As quite a private person, I found it daunting to open up in that way. But I was totally convinced that I had to get people to understand that in an organic organization, an organization that isn't just driven by the rules and formal lines of communication, you have to bring the whole person into the equation."

For the previous five years, Sands had played a supporting role to Mervyn Davies, his predecessor as CEO. "Mervyn set a very clear tone. He's a fantastic people person, an obsessive communicator, and paid special attention to the cultural side of this place," Sands explained. "I was very conscious in taking on the leadership mantle from him that I needed to continue building on the things he had been so effective at, but to find my own way to do it."

Sands felt his initial move had to send a message: at a meeting convened specifically to talk about the creation of financial value, he therefore deliberately chose to begin by addressing the human and cultural dimension.

Sands and other higher-ambition leaders see business performance and the health of the organization as inextricably linked. They pursue a simultaneous solve that will deliver superior outcomes to all key stakeholders, including employees, shareholders, customers, suppliers, and the communities they serve. And they recognize the demands that places on their own leadership for creating a level of connection and trust with each of these constituencies, which depends on their own capacity to bring their whole person into the equation.

In this chapter, we will use the story of SCB to provide an integrated view of how all these dimensions connect in action. We will show how higher-ambition leaders like Sands deliver superior economic and social value by simultaneously solving the challenges of developing business strategy, delivering performance, nurturing the organization's culture, and providing the individual and collective leadership required. We will then explore each of those elements in subsequent chapters.

The "Banana Skin" Bank

In 2010, Sands was heading a very successful international bank. In less than a decade, from late 2001, when Davies took over as CEO, to 2010, SCB's assets and profits had grown fourfold. The bank was positioned in attractive, high-growth markets in Asia, Africa, and the Middle East. It had become the favored employer for some of the most talented people in the financial industry and had helped restore the sight of more than 2.5 million blind or partially sighted people around the world (more on that later). What's more, it had weathered the 2008 to 2009 financial crisis more successfully than virtually all its peers, without relying on any emergency government or central bank funding, for reasons that have to do with the distinctive, higher-ambition approach Davies and Sands had pursued over the previous six years.

In 2002, however, when Sands joined SCB, few people could believe the bank had such potential. SCB had long been a midtier player that struggled to compete with the world's largest financial institutions, a perennial takeover target, an inconsistent financial performer, and a company that even its own employees viewed as average. "We were definitely a mediocre bank," Sands told us. "Our own people thought so." Many outsiders agreed. The bank had gotten into enough scrapes and near-death experiences over the years that the press sometimes referred to SCB as the "banana skin" bank because it always seemed to be slipping up. The bank had narrowly avoided a takeover by Lloyds Bank in 1986, suffered heavy losses at the end of the eighties, been badly hit by a stockbroking scandal in India in 1991, and survived another takeover attempt by Barclays in 1998.

In 1998, under the leadership of a new CEO, Rana Talwar, the bank embarked on a strategy of growth through acquisition, which made some sense because that is exactly how the bank had historically been built. After its founding in 1853 as the Chartered Bank, the firm had meandered and merged its way into markets throughout southern and eastern Asia, Africa, and the Gulf. It had only become Standard Chartered Bank in 1969, when the Chartered Bank merged with the Standard Bank of South Africa, which itself had grown through acquisition, notably of the Bank of West Africa Limited, which had branches in Nigeria, Ghana, Sierra Leone, and Gambia.

From 1998 to 2000, Talwar, in collaboration with then-chairman Sir Patrick Gillam, stepped up the acquisition activity. The bank purchased the non-Swiss trade finance business of UBS, the Thai retail bank Nakornthon, the Metropole Bank in Lebanon, and, in 2000, acquired the India-based Grindlays unit of ANZ Banking Group for $1.3 billion. By 2002, SCB could boast that it was the largest foreign-owned bank in India (by virtue of the Grindlays acquisition), was among the top-three biggest financial institutions in China, operated hundreds of branches in South Korea and throughout Indonesia, and maintained a presence in dozens of markets from the Falkland Islands to Botswana to Nepal.

The acquisitions bulked up the bank, built its assets, and extended its reach. For the five years prior to Sands's arrival, the bank had increased its total assets from $77 billion in 1997 to $107 billion in 2001. The number of customer accounts had risen, too, during the same period, from just over 45 million to almost 68 million. But growth on so many fronts also brought increasing debate and conflict over direction. "There was a feeling of organizational drift," Sands told us. "No sense of a top team. If you talked with people around the group, you would get a very different take on the priorities. There was a lot of politics at the top. There were a lot of cynical people at the bank."

Profits and earnings told a disappointing story. Operating profits had been up and down during that five-year period, as had earnings per share, and were on a downward slide in 2002. "We were known as the 'jam tomorrow' bank," Sands said—always promising better results down the road, but never quite delivering.

Another factor added to the sense of malaise: while SCB had been not quite managing to deliver, Citigroup and HSBC had been building huge, well-oiled banking machines that were rolling across the world. HSBC, in 2001, had net revenue of $26 billion compared to SCB's $4.5 billion, $700 billion in total assets compared to SCB's $107 billion, and posted an operating profit of over $11 billion, while SCB had earned just over $1 billion. Citigroup was also a far larger and more successful financial institution than SCB. Citigroup was formed from the merger of Citicorp and Travelers Group in 1998, and it registered net revenue of almost $84 billion in 2002 and employed almost ten times as many people as did SCB: 259,000 to 29,000. In 2002, SCB's fifty-one countries looked rather meager in comparison to HSBC, which had operations in eighty countries, and Citi, with branches in over one hundred. It seemed only too likely that one of these two giants of international banking would finally finish the job that Lloyds Bank and Barclays had failed to get done earlier: swallow up the smaller player, assimilate its operations, and take down the Standard Chartered signs on its branches around the world.

In 2001, the board dismissed Talwar and replaced him with Mervyn Davies. Davies, in turn, reached out to Sands, who had been consulting with SCB for several years, to join as finance director. Sands had recently been promoted to director at McKinsey & Company, the management consultancy. "Very few people leave at that point," Sands told us. Why would they? A McKinsey director looks forward to a relatively clear career path that involves engagement and influence with the leading companies of the world, and considerable reputation, wealth, and business leadership. "But I thought that, rather than getting even better at making violins as a craftsman at McKinsey, this was an opportunity to have a completely new adventure," said Sands.

Like all the higher-ambition CEOs in our sample, Sands was able to sense the potential of SCB and to genuinely believe it could be realized. "I had a sense of Standard Chartered as being an institution that had great promise," Sands said. "But it had not quite worked out the formula for delivering on that promise. I also thought that the leadership team—Mervyn and the others on the board—was a group of people who could actually unlock its potential. And there are very few opportunities you get in life to walk into a situation like that."

In essence, Sands saw an opportunity to achieve his own personal higher ambitions. As Sands explained to us, "Fundamentally, what drives me is to shape the organization simultaneously to be very effective in terms of performance, a great place to work, and something that is actually a force for good."

Turn Over Every Rock

The task for the new leadership team was clear. Davies convened an emergency session with the bank's top 250 managers and asked Sands to present on strategy. Sands put it bluntly: "I said, 'The strategy is very simple. We've just got to perform. That's all our strategy is. We have no other strategy.'" Sands stressed the precariousness of the bank's position. "If we didn't sort it out, we would get taken over," he told us.

Clearly, the bank had to do better at creating financial value. To reinforce the message, Davies and Sands had the bank's managers hear their shareholders' perspectives directly. "We got analysts and investors to talk to the top three hundred or four hundred people," Sands recalled. "The investors were seriously pissed off. Part of the problem was nobody had actually been listening to what they were complaining about." In addition to the languishing share price, the investors were not happy with the bank's inefficient capital structure. "We were bleeding money," Sands said, "and nobody had really paid attention to it."

"Mervyn and I were very clear on what we had to do first," Sands told us. "It was costs, risk, the basics of the P&L, revenue, sorting out the capital structure." Davies and Sands reviewed every country and operation in the portfolio in terms of risk, revenue, and potential. "It was turn over every rock and sort out stuff," Sands said.

One of their early moves was to cut back on the use of outside consultants. Sands had to personally approve every consulting contract with a value of $25,000 or more (small potatoes by the standards of a major international consulting firm). This was noteworthy not only because of Sands's background with McKinsey, but also because of what it said about how the bank was to be managed. For a management team that had long relied on consultants, the cutback sent the message: from now on, we make our own decisions about who we are and what we're going to do.

Davies and Sands also sought to reset expectations about performance. They reviewed every one of the top one hundred managers: about thirty left the bank, voluntarily or involuntarily. It was not a purge, exactly, but a significant and unmistakable signal that they were setting a new standard.

The management pair also reviewed the entire portfolio of the bank's holdings and businesses. As they studied what they had, the patchwork of businesses made less and less sense to them, and they set about defining, focusing, and paring the portfolio, a process that took about a year to complete. When the two were done, SCB had eliminated its underperforming assets and businesses and focused on markets that were already profitable or where they believed they could become profitable. It was clear that SCB was no longer a global emerging-markets bank, but instead focused on three geographies: Asia, Africa, and the Middle East. These were areas where the bank had institutional history, deep local knowledge, and strong relationships—meaningful sources of competitive advantage—that, fortuitously, also included the fastest-growing parts of the world.

Develop a Strong/Strong Organizing Model

So far, the actions of SCB might seem like scenes from a pretty typical turnaround story. Pare back to the profitable assets, raise performance expectations, weed out nonperformers. What Sands emphasized next, however, is interesting, and opens a window onto the approach of higher-ambition leaders. He described a strategy that was based on a strong/strong approach to combining global scale with deep local knowledge that competitors would find hard to match. He also talked about the culture and people strategies that would enable that organizational model to be successful. He stressed the importance of making explicit commitments to all the key stakeholders. And he described the value of putting it all in a simple document to communicate across the entire bank and externally, so that everyone could understand it and be held accountable, from the leadership team down, for living up to their commitments.

"We weren't through the woods yet, because there was a big bankruptcy crisis in Hong Kong, so we were under pretty interesting performance pressure at the time," Sands said. "But we could see that the fundamentals were getting there. And we thought, 'Well, we'd better work out what we want to be when we grow up.' So we decided to do some work on a strategic vision. I've spent a huge amount of time on it, working with Mervyn in particular, but also the team as a whole." In addition to the management team, they also held focus groups and shared drafts with a broader range of managers. The final draft became known as "Leading the Way."

The document started with a bold aspiration: to be the best international bank. It then defined three key aspects of SCB's strategic approach. The first derived from the asset review: that SCB would focus on attractive, growing markets where it could leverage its relationships and expertise. The second was that the bank would win in those markets by combining global capability with deep local knowledge to outperform competitors. The third aspect—which sought to avoid the trap that SCB had fallen into during the previous five years—was that SCB would maintain management discipline, balancing the pursuit of growth with firm control of costs.

Combining strong global capability with strong local knowledge has long been considered the holy grail of international banking, so SCB was hardly original in this regard. However, neither of the bank's two larger competitors, HSBC and Citi, had been able to achieve this. "HSBC has traditionally had strong country CEOs and weak global lines of business," Sands explained. Citi, by contrast, has been known for building strong lines of business across all geographies, but with relatively weak country leaders.

"We decided we wanted a model in which both roles are strong," Sands said. The leadership team wanted to foster debate and to even encourage "friction between the CEOs and business heads." Unlike its big competitors, SCB did not want to compromise by settling for either of the weak/strong solutions. "We didn't want to be in a situation where we're always doing something that is nearly as good as HSBC or Citi," Sands said. "That's not the aspiration." The aspiration was to be the best international bank.

To achieve the strong/strong organizational model, Davies and Sands embarked on a process of restructuring. From the agglomeration of country operations, they streamlined the organization into two businesses: whole-sale and consumer. They organized the geographies into two regions—Asia, and Middle East/Africa/the West. "And then we have six or seven functions, which are organized on a global basis. There was quite a lot of work involved in putting that model into place," Sands told us, "because it wasn't as clean as that."

At the country level, Davies and Sands upgraded the role of the CEOs, giving them more autonomy and decision-making power, particularly over two important dimensions of the business: governance and country rela-tionships. This increase in authority enabled the CEOs to deal directly with an important group of stakeholders, the local regulators, and generally play a much more active role in the development of local capital markets and credit bureaus. In such dealings, representatives of large international banks often seek to find ambiguities and opportunities in the local regula-tions that they can manipulate or exploit for the bank's gain. SCB did not take this approach. Instead, SCB's strategy was to become a "trusted in-sider." "We try to play a very responsible role," Sands observed. If the regu-lators view the country CEOs as financial carpetbaggers, "that does have a price, in terms of the way governments and regulators will look at you when you try to do things in their markets."

Even as Davies and Sands were building the role of the country CEOs, they also worked to strengthen the bank's business lines across geogra-phies. To do so, they needed their people to reach out and find opportuni-ties to conduct more business across country borders and boundaries. To encourage such behavior, SCB's Wholesale Banking division instituted a new, unusual incentive. The leader of the local wholesale business would receive credit for any business that his locally based customer booked, even if the booking was made in a different geographic area.

So, while the CEO of SCB Korea would be worrying primarily about the overall profitability of his country operation, Sands explained, "the Wholesale Banking guy will be managing the global relationship with a client like Samsung. We don't want him to worry about whether deals are done domestically with a client or internationally." This meant that the SCB business manager could take a less parochial view and leverage SCB's greatest competitive advantage for its customers. "Big local banks can do stuff locally," Sands explained. "What they can't do is all the international stuff, which we can do incredibly well."

The result is that the bank's management can focus on trade investment corridors and the important players that operate within them. "We probably know as much as anybody knows about China's relationship with Africa," Sands said, "because we've been involved in many of the major deals between China and Africa." Very few banks have the ability to serve both ends of these complex investment corridors. "We've spent a lot of time focusing on those and working out how to pull the team together to serve them," he said. That ability to bring to bear local knowledge all along an international investment line is a clear point of differentiation for SCB.

But the strong global/strong local organizing model, although strategically attractive, is not as simple to implement as it may sound. Sands argued for the benefits of tension and even conflict between country and global business lines, but there are some places where conflict can be problematic, one of which is the balance sheet. "This is the place where the two businesses have to come together, and the country perspective is important," Sands told us. "Even if you have two businesses in a country, you only have one balance sheet." A review of the country operations showed that there was much dysfunctional behavior in reconciling the balance sheet and not enough expertise within the local country operations to manage the process. So SCB created a new corporate entity, a balance-sheet review team, that would visit the country operations—particularly the smaller ones—and essentially show them "this is how you should be doing it."

While introducing a corporate perspective helped reduce some of the conflict, the balance-sheet review team still had to approach the work with sensitivity to the local ways of managing disagreement. "What would count as robust discussion in an American company might be unacceptable here," Sands said. "You could have the same substantive discussion, but you've got to do it in a way that is culturally sensitive. You can't have people losing face."

Establishing and maintaining short lines of communication helped the bank manage the complexities and tensions of implementing the strong global business/strong local geography model. "The feel of being a fairly small company helped," Sands explained, "because it helped people to get on the phone and talk to each other and work out how to quickly turn around a deal."

Top management modeled the culture of direct communications. While most banks are notorious for elaborate hierarchies and formal chains of command, Sands told us, "Mervyn catalyzed a culture of direct communications. I get e-mails from individuals all around the bank all the time, on all sorts of topics. I can have a substantive e-mail dialogue with somebody four or five levels down in one of the businesses, and nobody feels threatened by that. That would never have happened before."

Similarly, leadership set an example for productively managing conflict. At the meetings of the group management committee, for example, "real debates happen," Sands said. "There is lots of disagreement and discussion. We all respect each other. Once we make decisions, we get on with it. You can't tell the organization to work in a certain way and then not do it from the top."

Dramatically Raise the Stakes of the Game

In 2004, with substantially improved performance, a well-articulated international insider strategy, and the distinctive strong/strong organizing model taking shape, Davies and Sands did what higher-ambition leaders do when they feel that the company is ready: they find some way to dramatically raise the stakes of the game, to take the company to a whole new level. "We were coming off the back of very, very strong underlying performance," Sands said. "The organization was working pretty well. And we've got a very good board whose attitude has tended to be that you've got to be bold. If you just stand still and tread water, you will get taken out. But as long as you continue to perform, that's not going to happen." The two started to think about what the next step might be, what the "next level" could look like.

They caught a glimpse of the future when an important opportunity arose toward the end of that year: a controlling stake in Korea First Bank (KFB) became available for acquisition in the fall of 2004. KFB was a major player in South Korea, with an overall 6 percent share of the market, 10 percent of the total number of bank branches, and 8 percent of Korea's mortgage market.

HSBC made a $3.1 billion bid to purchase KFB, and the bank, along with the market, expected the deal would be closed by the end of December. But SCB was quietly mobilizing its forces. Its long history in South Korea put the bank in good stead. "One of the things we've learned is about laying foundations in countries," Sands explained, and SCB had laid its foundations in Korea well. "We had had a wholesale banking operation there since the sixties. We launched a consumer banking operation to learn about the consumer bank. We actually bought a stake in another bank. Having done all that, having built relationships with the regulators, by the time we got to what was then Korea First Bank, we knew exactly what questions to ask."

SCB's strong global business/strong local geography model, use of direct communications, and open leadership style were also key. The streamlined organization with a clear geographic focus (Asia, Africa, and the Middle East) and two businesses (Wholesale and Consumer Banking) enabled Davies and Sands to keep well informed and to move rapidly. "We could work very, very quickly on due diligence. And we took some very specific risks as well, in due diligence. My understanding," Sands told us, "is that HSBC found it more difficult to take those risks, because those decisions were getting pushed up and down."

On Christmas Eve 2004, Davies and Sands made an eleventh hour move. They decided that KFB was worth more and upped the offer to $3.3 billion. The money markets were closed through January 14. But Davies and Sands had to prove that SCB had the money to do the deal, which, in fact, it did not. Nor could they go to the markets to get assurances that the money would be available when the markets reopened in January. Davies and Sands decided to personally guarantee the funds. "Effectively, we did a deal to do a deal," Sands explained, "and then we announced the deal on January 11, and when the markets were open again, we raised the money. Mervyn and I would have had to have gone if we didn't do the deal by January 14." Just as they pledged, Davies and Sands were able to raise the money they needed for the purchase by issuing $2 billion in new shares and drawing on other available funds.

The acquisition marked an important turning point for SCB. "Up until that point, I think a lot of external people wondered whether we were really a player," Sands said. "Then we suddenly stole Korea First from under HSBC's nose. We did a $3.3 billion acquisition, three times as big as anything we'd ever done before. And that changed the external mind-set around Standard Chartered. There's no doubt that The City [of London] community, investors, our competitors started looking at us differently. And that had a huge impact on our organization, because we realized that we were serious about taking on these much, much bigger organizations."

The boldness of the KFB acquisition actually increased the imperative for SCB to continue to raise its game. The bank was still a midtier player, well positioned in the world's most attractive markets, and would rapidly become a tantalizing takeover target if it stumbled. "We're constantly trying to step up the pace of the organization," Sands emphasized, "the pace at which we make decisions, the pace at which we implement, the pace at which we grow. If we can't simplify the way we do things, there will be too much drag on the organization."

In particular, Davies and Sands sought to move even further away from the centralized decision making that had characterized their first two years. "We acknowledged the fact that we pulled everything into the center and micromanaged," Sands said. "Now we're trying to push it back out again."

Sands came to see the recruitment and development of talent as fundamental to this effort and to further strengthening both sides of the strong/strong model. In the process, he had to revise the assumptions he had long operated under at McKinsey. "As a consultant, you tend to be working on finding the right answer and how you go about doing it," he told us. "What I've increasingly realized is that's completely useless if you don't have the people." Now Sands sees business problems quite differently. "With any business issue, about 10 percent of the problem is working out *what* to do about it. The next 25 percent is working out *how* to do that. The remaining 65 percent of the problem is working out *who* is going to do it," he said.

"The thing I'm most concerned about," Sands told us, "is building leadership capacity." As a consequence, Sands has paid a great deal of attention to attracting, educating, and managing talent across the organization, such as relaunching SCB's international MBA program. The focus started when Sands was working with Davies. For example, they developed an unusual initiative specifically designed to attract people with talents and expertise who might not show up through the conventional recruiting channels.

They created Project Istanbul (which actually has nothing to do with the country of Turkey or its capital city) to bring in "young Turks"—that is, bold, bright talents who had not been part of the banking world.

"We made a curious proposition to these people," Sands said. "Mervyn and I would interview them, and we'd say, 'We're going to pay you less than you have been paid or could get paid, and we don't know what job you're going to do, but join us, because you'll love it here.' And this seemed to work quite well, rather to our surprise." Sands laughed. "It hasn't been huge in numbers. But actually, in terms of an injection of ambitious, smart, different mind-set people, it was extraordinarily valuable."

Just as important as recruitment, of course, is the development of people already in place. "It's often about unlocking people you've got," Sands said. "Working out how to put them in a different place, or help them build on strengths they've got that they haven't quite realized how to use."

Movement also strengthens collaboration. "We move people across the dimensions, because when you're an international organization, making your matrix work well is critical. We take a lot of risks in moving people out of functional silos," Sands told us. "We appointed a head of legal and compliance who at one point ran the credit card business. He was not a lawyer, he was not a compliance expert, but he understood our business. And we put a CEO in China who actually had run the organizational learning group. She was not a career banker at all. The more you can get people to work in different dimensions of the matrix, the less 'siloed' they become."

Movement and the resultant networking, in turn, underpin a culture where knowledge sharing and collaboration can become a norm. "We expect professionals to make a contribution to the institution, as well as to their own area of responsibility," Sands said. "We designate 'global products' and push those across geographies. And we offer incentives for pulling in other people's ideas, as well as for propagating their own ideas."

Reinforce the Cultural Glue

For a numbers guy and a banker, a former financially focused consultant and a zealot for performance, Sands spent a lot of time talking with us about a rather unexpected topic: how much fun he has in his position as CEO, and how much fun the bank's employees, in general, derive from their work. Much of that fun seems to come from a genuine enjoyment they take in each other and their relationships. "People get passionate about this organization," Sands said. "The cultural side of this place is very special. This is one of Mervyn's great achievements and legacies. Mervyn found ways of unleashing, reinforcing, fueling the cultural glue and excitement of the place."

"We are extraordinarily diverse," Sands said. "And all of us enjoy the diversity of the organization." It has taken a lot of time and work, and many initiatives and activities, to reach the point where diversity is seen as a source of strength and even delight, rather than a cause of disconnection and tension. Much of the success comes from understanding the differences in cultures and accepting the practices and traditions of each. This comes down to things that may seem simple, but have symbolic cultural value. For example, Sands has his sober, low-key London office regularly inspected by feng shui consultants to make sure that the right positive energy flows. The bank celebrates Diwali, the Indian festival of lights, as well as the Chinese New Year. It is careful about scheduling meetings or events on Friday, because Friday is part of the Islamic weekend, and has been offering Islamic banking (a major issue because the Koran forbids the payment or collection of interest on loans) since 1993.

"We do a lot of things to celebrate our cultural diversity," Sands said. "For example, the 'Dance Idol' competition."

"The what?" Nathaniel asked. Sands seemed pleased to have caused his interviewers some bemusement.

"Dance Idol," he repeated, and explained that the bank challenged those in the country organizations to form dance teams, with a minimum of four and a maximum of thirty people each. The teams had to devise a dance that was related in some way to SCB's strategy, surely one of the more intriguing assignments that any choreographer might face. Competitions were held in various locations around the world and proved wildly popular. A hundred dance teams entered from India alone. "It was about letting people understand each other a little bit and celebrate each other's culture," Sands said.

Much of the success of celebrating and leveraging diversity at SCB stems from the ability to read, understand, and accept cultural differences. You have to be "conscious of the way people are approaching problems and thinking about them, and their way of articulating things, and knowing what's not being said," Sands told Nathaniel and Tobias. "A very classic Asian thing to do, if they disagree with you, is to defer the problem and then disagree with you later. So what you need to do is tease out the disagreement there and then. We have many different cultures within Africa. You shouldn't work on the assumption that you immediately understand exactly what is being meant by what people say. You need to work a little harder in the communication in the conversations. The underlying respect and way you treat people are incredibly important."

Some people, according to Sands, are not able to catch or embrace the differences: "We hired one person, a very nice guy, but it just didn't seem to work. It wasn't because he was nasty. He just couldn't read the room, which meant he was constantly getting into misunderstandings with his teams and his peers. And we couldn't work out how to help him crack it."

SCB's creative approaches to cultural integration are not just fun but a source of competitive advantage, because they help the bank gain the fullest possible value from its acquisitions. When the bank acquired additional operations in Pakistan and Taiwan (in each case, as the first international bank the national regulator trusted enough to allow to make a local acquisition), it conducted a "welcome week" across the entire organization with a series of events focused on Pakistan and Taiwan. "We wanted every country in the group to know what it was that we had bought, and why, and also to do some sort of celebration, based on food or clothing or something to do with the cultures. They weren't new countries to us, but we've increased their importance," said Sands.

The bank also dispatched ambassadors from these countries to operations throughout the world. Sixty Taiwanese employees visited thirty countries to conduct events with bank staff and with members of the local business communities. In addition to teaching the other countries about Taiwan, the Taiwanese learned a great deal about the bank. Sands explained, "The idea was that these people would go back to Taiwan and talk about what they'd learned from Uganda, or what it's like there. But actually the meta-message is all about the family. It's all about the organization they've become part of."

According to Sands, the process of building a shared sense of community—even across diversity—is critical "because a lot of what happens when you grow is you end up building semi-independent entities that aren't actually part of the same seamless whole." Sands spoke of the evolution in his own thinking: "I came from the numerical, analytical side of consulting. But I spend a huge amount of my time now worrying about culture, because I want to make sure that, as we grow and evolve, we don't lose what's made us special." For example, once a month Sands does a "thematic call" with a specific group within the bank. "It will be partly me talking, but it will partly be structured questions, too. People will have submitted questions, we'll get them on the live line, they'll ask me questions," he explained. One call took place on International Women's Day with four hundred up-and-coming women across the group. "Ten of them were on live lines asking me questions about what we were doing about flexible working and particular issues around international mobility for women," said Sands. He did another call for the fiftieth anniversary of Ghana's independence and one for the anniversary of the acquisition of the Korea First Bank.

The "Seeing Is Believing" Initiative

Another reinforcement for the cultural glue is the involvement of SCB employees in their communities through various social and charitable activities. "There's a very strong community aspect here," Sands said. But when he first joined the bank, the community activities were highly localized and personalized. "We were doing all this community stuff all over the place, and it was all subscale," he said.

Just as it refocused its business portfolio, SCB refocused its corporate charitable-giving activities. In 2003, Davies launched a corporate-wide initiative, "Seeing Is Believing," as a way to celebrate the one hundred-fiftieth anniversary of the bank. "We thought it would be nice to save the sight of one person for every staff member," Sands told us. "We had twenty-eight thousand people in the organization, so we thought we'd raise enough money to save the sight of twenty-eight thousand people."

To pursue this goal, SCB created Seeing Is Believing in partnership with the International Association for the Prevention of Blindness. Its mission is to provide eye-care access to people around the world and, in particular, to alleviate the problems associated with preventable or reversible blindness.

The project was a success from the start. With fund-raising support from SCB staff in its first year, Seeing Is Believing successfully raised $1.6 million to fund fifty-six thousand sight restorations, twice its goal. "We overdelivered," said Sands. "We thought, well, that's very interesting. Let's go for a million people over three years. Our target was to do it by World Sight Day, October 2007. We hit that. We've now said, 1 million is a good thing, but the problem is still very big. There are 45 million blind people in the world, 36 million of whom don't need to be. Let's go for 10 million, because then you're actually making a real impact on the problem." By the end of 2009, SCB had restored the sight of over 2.5 million people across its markets.

SCB has raised a great deal of money for its partner organizations; it has also put its human assets to work on the problem, particularly its skilled bankers. Sands told us that the donation of operations expertise is just as important as donating money or advising on how to raise money. "The issue with doing philanthropic work was helping the NGOs have the capability to deliver the services in the markets in a scalable fashion," Sands told us. "Our guys locally have gotten involved in helping with the financial management and providing support to the NGOs, particularly in places like Africa and Bangladesh."

Sands noted that the Seeing Is Believing program has been good not just for the world and the people who have been helped, but also for SCB. The program has unleashed huge amounts of energy and has created a model that he uses to raise managers' aspirations. He explained, "We went from having a lot of subscale, well-meaning initiatives to doing something that really makes a difference. By concentrating resources, being focused, and being ambitious, we can do the same in our businesses." It has also reinforced the sense of community across the bank. "People in Sierra Leone did a sponsored walk that raised, in the scheme of things, not a huge amount of money," Sands said. "But it's the idea that the people in Sierra Leone are raising money for eyesight in Bangladesh."

Weathering the Financial Crisis: Standing by SCB's Clients

In 2008 and 2009, the collapse of the world's financial markets subjected leading financial institutions to unprecedented levels of stress. SCB's largest competitor, Citibank, teetered on the brink, with its share price plunging from a high of over $50 per share in 2007 to under $1 in early 2009. But SCB came through with flying colors, outperforming its peers, and posting an unbroken record of income and profit growth throughout the crisis, without any reliance on emergency government or central bank funding.

"Part of our success," Sands explained, "was our geographic focus, and the way we ran our business model in terms of the amount of liquidity we have, the amount of capital we have, and the way we think about risk." But major reasons for SCB's success were also the distinctive organizational and leadership approaches that Davies and Sands had pursued over the previous six years.

In reflecting on what had carried them through unscathed, Sands named four key points: "First is that we have a very clear strategy and we stuck to it. Everybody understood it, and we were very, very focused." This was in marked contrast to the institutions that got into the deepest trouble. "If you look at what went wrong with a lot of banks," Sands pointed out, "it was on the periphery of strategy; it was where people were doing things that were a little bit offbeat."

Second, Sands continued, "it is deep within the culture of the bank to focus on the basics—the operational detail, the granularity of what we do in managing capital, liquidity, and risks, control of costs." Sands connected this to the bank's distinctive approaches to talent: "We call it 'swooping and soaring.' If you're a leader in the bank, you have to be able to swoop down to the six-inch level. You have to be able to crawl over the documentation of certain sorts of contracts, or the operational procedures and key control standards of certain types of activities. But you also need to be able to soar, which is to provide your team with the broader context so they understand how what they're doing fits into the broader picture, of either the bank strategy or the macro context." During the crisis, this expectation meant that senior people got deeply involved in the detail of what was going on and how to resolve it. "I don't think you would find that was true at all the other banks," Sands commented.

Third, Sands told us, "we stayed open for business." That is, the bank continued lending. Many of SCB's bankers saw the crisis as a huge opportunity to win new clients, given that most other banks had stopped making new loans. But Sands and the bank's senior leaders decided differently. "We decided we didn't want to take on new clients," Sands told us. "This ran counter to what many people thought within the bank and created tension in the organization."

But Sands and his team stood firm. "We basically said, 'No, we're going to focus all our capital, liquidity, and resources on supporting our existing clients.'"

Sands characterized that decision as a moment of truth: "We didn't have limitless capital. We didn't want to diffuse that across whatever we thought was the best idea or what could bring in a new client. We wanted it very, very focused on our existing client base."

The decision sent a powerful message to SCB's clients about the bank's commitment to them. "Our view," Sands explained, "is that clients have very long memories, and how you work with them during a crisis is what they will remember." The commitment has paid off in deeper client relationships. "The prize for us," Sands told us, "from a strategic point of view, was building deeper relationships with our clients, as opposed to trying to win more new clients. And that is exactly what we've done." Sands referred to the financial data as a proxy for the depth of the relationships. "If you compare 2008, 2009, and 2010, the number of clients with whom we made more than \$5 million and the number of clients with whom we made more than \$10 million both grew markedly."

The fourth reason for SCB's success during hard financial times, according to Sands, was the strength of the bank's values and culture. "Every team involved in banking came under huge pressure when the crisis hit. There were lots of fires breaking out all over the place, and it was a real test of the way an organization works," he said. The way the bank responded revealed deep cultural strengths. "Bad news traveled fast. People were very quick to make sure that we knew what was going on and where things were getting difficult." In addition, Sands noted, "People did the right thing for the bank. They realized that, in an environment like that, the important thing was that you didn't think about your particular business unit, or your particular part. You had to do the right thing for the bank, the right thing for the client." There was also an enormous amount of collaboration. "Virtual teams were springing up all over the place, dealing with this or that particular issue," said Sands.

Sands believed that this was very different from the way other banks operated through the downturn: "If you talk to people about the way other organizations were operating at the time, you hear about dysfunctional teams, people protecting their own area, frictions. It's just the way organizations performed under acute, acute stress and information overload. These were incredibly intense periods of time."

These cultural distinctions translated into operational advantages. "Often you have a lot of decisions that are being made around the deployment of capital or resources, which look very different from different perspectives," said Sands. What differentiates performance, he explained, is "the ability to stop and say, 'Hang on, this looks obvious from my perspective, but maybe I should talk to someone else and see whether it really works that way if looked at from a bigger-picture point of view.'" The bias to explore other perspectives must, of course, be coupled with the intention and ability to act quickly on what is learned. "That requires a very flexible communications and decision-making environment," he said. Formalized consultation and decision-making processes can act as impediments to speedy action.

Conclusion

SCB has created impressive economic value under the leadership of Davies and Sands. Profit before taxes, for example, grew from $1.3 billion in 2002, to $3.2 billion in 2006, and $5.2 billion in 2009. The bank expanded from twenty-nine thousand employees in 2002 to more than seventy-seven thousand employees in 2009.

How did SCB go from a mediocre, "banana skin" bank to one that not only survived the crisis but turned it to its advantage? How did Sands build on the foundations laid by Davies to unlock the promise and the potential that they both saw in SCB? Perhaps we should return to the story that opened this chapter—of Sands starting a corporate meeting with a picture of his childhood nanny's daughter. Why was it so important to him to present such a personal portrait of himself to his audience? What had he learned about leadership, about the culture, and about his own ambitions in the years since he had first served the company as a numbers-oriented consultant?

SCB achieved success in large part by focusing on social value as well as economic value. Sands came to understand that the quality of relationships and a diverse culture were key to SCB's ability to attract and retain distinctive talent. In turn, the capacity to work across cultures and boundaries and to engage conflict productively underpinned SCB's ability to create strong global lines of business, support strong country CEOs, and pursue a strategy that enabled customers to work the trade corridors between geographic areas where the competition may have had a physical presence but had less ability to collaborate than did SCB.

With this strong/strong organizing model, the bank achieved a best-of-both strategy of global capability and deep local knowledge. Dramatic improvements in financial performance coupled with bold strategic moves like the Korea First acquisition bolstered the belief that SCB had a winning team and strengthened pride and the sense of a shared community. Initiatives such as Seeing Is Believing increased employee commitment and the feeling of companywide purpose, while also improving the bank's reputation and credibility in the communities in which it operates. Commitment to existing customers during the financial crisis deepened relationships, built trust, and contributed to greater bank profitability.

We found that higher-ambition leaders like Sands have an intuitive ability to achieve this kind of simultaneous solve—the unique alignment among strategy, organization, and culture that most powerfully delivers superior economic and social value. Having focused in this chapter on the interconnections among these dimensions, in part II we will explore in more detail each of the disciplines—strategy, performance, community, and leadership—that constitute the distinctive work of higher-ambition leaders.

Part Two

The Disciplines of Higher-Ambition Leadership

Forging Strategic Identity

If the best and the brightest of one generation—in any generation, in any country—get together into one company ... then there's a feeling that, gee, we can do something really good.

—Jorma Ollila, Nokia

L IKE ALL GENERAL MANAGERS, higher-ambition CEOs face the challenge of creating sustained competitive advantage. However, we found that these leaders are distinctive in their realization that they cannot divorce a firm's strategy from the sensibilities and passions of its people. The story of Nokia illustrates how one of the higher-ambition leaders in our study, Jorma Ollila, helped that company return from the brink of extinction by forging a new, more powerful understanding of its distinctive character and unique capabilities to create economic and social value, what we think of as its fundamental *strategic identity*.

In the fall of 1991, Nokia was in tough shape. "This was not a company that was supposed to survive," said Ollila, Nokia's former CEO, during a conversation with Flemming Norrgren and Tobias Fredberg at the company's offices in Espoo, outside Helsinki. Finland, where Nokia is based, wasn't in much better condition at the time. "Finland, as an economy, was a basket case," Ollila told us, speaking in English in his deliberate, thought-ful way. "Everybody was thinking, 'This is soon going to be a forgotten hinterland.'"

But Ollila had no intention of letting that happen to his company or, if he could help it, to his country. In Finland, company and country are tightly associated. Finland has had a long struggle to establish its national identity. Little Finnish literature of note was published before the nineteenth century, and the country was long a part of Sweden, before becoming a grand duchy under Russian rule. It declared independence in 1917 and bitterly resisted invasion by the Soviet Union during World War II, but had to cede substantial territory. In this context, Nokia, in particular, has played the role of a Finnish national champion. Founded and led by families considered to be of true Finnish provenance, Nokia has been a perennial export leader. Ollila himself hails from an old, prominent Finnish family.

While others viewed Nokia as a failed company in a troubled economy, Ollila saw potential and unbounded opportunity instead. In our conversation with Ollila, he explained how he and his team set out on a journey of transformation that, at its core, involved crafting and then capitalizing on a new strategic identity. His reflections bear remarkable similarities to the stories we heard from the other CEOs in our sample. To a degree that struck us as genuinely distinctive, these leaders:

- *Craft a strategic identity that connects head, hands, and heart.*
  Through an intuitive, iterative, broadly engaging process, higher-ambition leaders define their firm's sense of strategic identity in a way that harnesses a distinctive core of people and capabilities (hands) to a meaningful purpose and core values (heart), and underpins a sustainable economic model (head). The extent of engagement involved in crafting a strategic identity strengthens the courage needed to follow through on the difficult decisions that the execution of the strategy may require.

- *See organizational capability as strategy.* Strategy and organization, for these leaders, are not separate domains. Rather, these leaders view superior organizational capability as a cornerstone of their strategy, and choices about organizing models as among their most strategic decisions.

- *Commit, yet adapt.* Higher-ambition leaders follow through, year after year, continuing to make investments that bring additional advantages or that leverage those advantages into new markets. Yet while emphasizing strategic consistency, they are highly attuned to the need to adapt and innovate continually. Many confronted difficult portfolio choices and spoke of the challenges of maintaining the social fabric and continuing to create a sense of shared identity and direction in the face of wrenching decisions.

Craft a Strategic Identity That Connects Head, Hands, and Heart

Until the early 1980s, if someone asked you to identify the core of the Nokia enterprise, you would probably have concluded that it was paper products or even rubber boots. Nokia is a conglomerate formed in 1967 through the merger of three venerable Finnish companies: Nokia Ab, a paper company, founded in 1865; Finnish Rubber Works, established in 1898; and Finnish Cable Works, founded in 1912. The conglomerate eventually comprised five main businesses—rubber, paper and forestry, wire cables, power generation, and electronics. The company's name comes from the nokia, a mink-like animal that dwells in the environs of the Nokianvirta River where the paper company established one of its early mills.

The late 1970s and early 1980s were exciting times for Nokia. The company's then CEO, Kari Kairamo, decided to push the company away from rubber boots and paper and toward the electronics and high-technology businesses that were taking off at the time. He used the profits from the company's legacy offerings, including the high-top Kontio rubber boots (a big seller), to make a series of acquisitions and investments, the largest ones in color television manufacturing and data systems. In 1982, most of the company's sales came from products like rubber boots and tissue paper. By 1988, electronics accounted for 60 percent of its sales, and Nokia had become Europe's third-largest producer of color televisions, with around 14 percent of the market.

The strategy was bold and high risk. Many of the acquired businesses had been struggling before Nokia purchased them, and Nokia had gambled that it could turn them around. In December 1988, Kairamo committed suicide, and in March 1989, Nokia reported that it had suffered a steep decline in profits relative to the previous year, almost entirely due to poor performance in the electronics division.

Turmoil in the business environment deepened Nokia's predicament. The Finnish economy was already struggling when the Soviet Union, which purchased as much as 20 percent of Finland's exports each year, collapsed. This, combined with weakening demand for television and video products in key European markets, dealt a body blow to Nokia and to the economy of Finland.

The new CEO, Simo Vuorilehto, was forced to undertake a substantial restructuring. Nokia sold its footwear operations to a management group and in November 1990 exited the tissue paper business. In early 1991, Nokia was in such disarray and uncertainty that the board sought help from an outside adviser. It commissioned a study of the company's strategic options by the European technology practice of a leading global management consultancy. The consultants spent several months studying Nokia's operations and opportunities and prepared a report they presented to the board in the fall of 1991.

A central issue that the consultants addressed was the future potential of Nokia's cell-phone business. As part of Kairamo's electronics push, in 1979, Nokia had entered a joint venture with Salora, a television maker, to develop radio telephones. In 1981, the Nordic Mobile Telephone (NMT), the first international mobile phone network, was established. Nokia introduced a car phone for the network in 1982 and brought its first portable phone to market in 1986. Meanwhile, in 1982, the European Conference of Postal and Telecommunications Administrations (CEPT) established a group to develop an international standard for mobile telephones, to be called GSM, the standard today. These moves and developments gave Nokia an early jump into the new and potentially exciting cell-phone industry. In 1988, it expanded its cordless phone operations by paying £2.5 million for a 25 percent stake in Shaye Communications, based in the United Kingdom. In February 1991, despite its financial and cash difficulties, Nokia bought Technophone, a British company. Suddenly, Nokia was the world's second-largest cell-phone company, after Motorola.

The consultants' report was not optimistic about Nokia's prospects. It said that Nokia was, in effect, a "hopeless" case and singled out the cell-phone business as a particularly "dubious" option. The consultants believed that Nokia did not have the basis for sustainable competitive advantage in cell phones and should, in fact, exit the business immediately. It is easy to understand why the consultants reached their conclusion: Nokia, struggling financially and on the periphery of major markets, appeared to lack the breadth and depth of the major telecommunications or electronics firms' resources.

"You could see that they thought they were very smart when they walked into the room," Ollila remembered, with his characteristic half-smile. But Ollila was having none of it. "I told some of the board members, 'If you believe these guys, go away. Because that's wrong.'"

The board nonetheless chose to heed the consultants' advice and offered Nokia's mobile division for sale at a knock-down valuation to Ericsson, the Swedish telecommunications company. Yet after two months of deliberations and evaluations, Ericsson dropped out and passed on the offer. "They said, 'We don't want to touch this thing,'" Ollila recounted.

The collapse of the sale left the board between a rock and a hard place. Rather than look for another buyer, it decided that perhaps Ollila was right. Maybe the mobile telephony business could form the core of the company's future strategy. Nokia was, after all, number two in mobile telephony worldwide—even if the market was small—and its revenues had been growing. "There were some people on the board of directors who said, 'Okay, the only thing is to get a bunch of young guys and see what we can do with this,'" Ollila told us. At the time, although Ollila was the head of the cellphone business, he did not expect to be the young guy the board would tap to run the entire company. In January 1992, the board appointed Ollila as Nokia's new president. "It was a surprise totally for everybody, including myself," Ollila told us. "A total generation change. Big risk."

A big risk, perhaps, but there were few other options. "People had already lost their money," Ollila said. Market capitalization had fallen to less than $1 billion. Nokia had to do something dramatic or it would very likely cease to exist.

The board's bet on the cell-phone business, which the consultants and Ericsson had shunned, and its choice of the leader of the cell-phone division to become president are particularly interesting because the directors were not especially well versed in the business. "There wasn't a single technologist on the board," Ollila said. There were insurance executives and bankers and directors from the old guard of Scandinavian business ownership, but no director who could have stepped forward to lead the company into the new era of technology.

Although Ollila had much more experience in the business than the directors did, he was not exactly a dyed-in-the-wool technologist either.

After earning a master's degree in political science from the University of Helsinki, a master's in science (economics) from the London School of Economics, and a master's in science (engineering) from Helsinki University of Technology, he had spent eight years at Citibank, holding various managerial positions within its corporate banking division. In 1986, he joined Nokia as senior vice president of finance and had only become president of Nokia cell phones in 1990. But Ollila had spent his two years learning everything he could about the design and manufacture of the product. "I went to the floor, to the factory, to the labs," he told us. "I spent two years learning."

Why, then, we asked Ollila, had he come to such a different conclusion than the consultants and Ericsson? Strategy making, he responded, involves not just rational analysis of markets and competitors, but also intangibles and, in particular, commitment: "Commitment determines the company's most fundamental questions of existence and survival." He continued, "I had an intuitive feeling, and there was a group of people whom I knew felt the same way. We saw the crisis as just pitiful mismanagement by the fifty- and sixty-year-olds—the old school." Like Conant and Sands with their respective businesses, Ollila sensed the potential of the mobile business and was willing to commit fully to it.

Behind his belief and commitment was a deep insight into the hidden strengths of the business that the consultants had missed. Ollila explained: "There was a group of 'youngsters' who had been with the company for ten or twenty years, not more, and who had been attracted to the company, typically in the early 1980s. What was remarkable about this group was that they were the best and brightest." He continued, "If the best and the brightest of one generation—in any generation, in any country—get together into one company, which happened to be Nokia, and many of them are in telecom, then there's a feeling that, gee, we can do something really good."

Embedded in this group's sense of itself was a different and more powerful strategic identity for the firm. These people represented, Ollila continued, "a nucleus of know-how in the mobile phone business. It's the cumulative knowledge of what you know when you're first here as a twenty-year-old in 1981, when cellular networks are just being invented, and then you are a thirty-year-old in 1991. You basically are the best in the world, if you are a smart guy. You have worked all your life, done your thesis in university. There literally were hundreds of these people. It was a fantastically strong core."

Having identified such promising potential, Ollila and his colleagues still had to unleash it. The emotions that the crisis triggered worked in their favor. Nokia's employees, especially that brilliant band of engineers, had been seriously roiled by the period of financial distress, bad press, and the company's near-sale to, and then maddening rejection by, Ericsson. Ollila told us that the Nokia engineers found the whole episode to be "shameful." Their pride had been battered, and they essentially said, "We really have to prove that we can do better." When the board of directors selected Ollila, the engineers cheered. "There was a really energizing feeling when they saw that there was somebody of their ilk becoming a CEO," said Ollila.

Ollila fueled that energy. Within weeks of his appointment, he went public with a bold vision for the company, predicting it would soon break into the Japanese market and that its cell-phone sales would grow by 30 percent to 40 percent per year for the rest of the decade.

More significantly, Ollila and his colleagues tapped into the already powerful sense of purpose that had motivated the engineers to join Nokia and work on mobile telephony in the first place. When Ollila had stepped in as head of the mobile phone division in 1990, his first focus had been profitability. "My first two years," he remembered, "I had to fire seven hundred fifty people. The business was not healthy." It had lost money each of the previous three years, as it expanded, according to Ollila, from a lab of four hundred people to an industrial enterprise. But by the summer of 1991, he and his team started thinking about what the business could become. "We didn't think about beating Motorola," he told us. "Motorola looked too far away and too big, too smart to think about what they did. So we didn't think about beating them. We thought about doing something significant that would have an impact and help us to grow a business."

From the beginning, there was talk of social value. "Making an impact, changing people's lives in how they communicate—that was always in our PowerPoint slides," Ollila said. "We wanted to change the world." In the spring of 1992, Nokia adopted a new theme, "Connecting People." "We really felt good about it. It struck a chord. We were proud that we had a theme that wasn't centering around technology," commented Ollila.

Nokia's theme put the mobile phone strategy in a whole new light, as both a business and a social endeavor. And it led the company's leaders to two assumptions that were fundamentally different from those of other players in the market at the time.

The first assumption was about who would be the ultimate customer for this new thing called the cell phone and how that person would use it. The conventional industry wisdom at the time was that the cell phone would always be a premium item, a toy for business executives. Nokia, however, in keeping with its "connecting people" theme, saw the cell phone as a way for people of all kinds to connect with one another quickly and easily, wherever they were. "There was a strong element of trying to figure out where is this world going with the communication?" Ollila said. "And there was both a utilitarian aspect—productivity improvement—as well as an entertainment or lifestyle aspect." Nokia believed that, if defined as both a practical and a lifestyle product, the phones would end up "in everybody's pocket." Like Microsoft's vision of a computer on every desk, Nokia saw ubiquity and ever-declining prices for its product.

This bold, contrarian assumption led to a second one that was perhaps even bolder. The companies that saw the cell phone as an executive toy naturally assumed that their biggest markets would be those with the highest concentration of executives, which meant the United States and Europe.

Nokia, however, "made an assumption that the winner in this game is not going to be decided in the U.S. or in the European market, but in the emerging markets," Ollila told us.

By the end of 1992, despite the consultants' earlier skeptical report, Ollila and the senior team were not leading Nokia's people on an irrational charge, but directing them to work toward the future potential—or, as Wayne Gretzky put it, to "skate to where the puck is going to be." They had developed an increasingly compelling strategic identity for the enterprise that connected the core engineering strengths of the organization (hands) to a meaningful purpose of connecting people that engendered emotional commitment (heart) and capitalized on a unique set of insights into the market dynamics and future sources of success (head). This strategic identity proved the basis for motivating and continuing to attract the best and the brightest, not only from Finland, but from the rest of the world as well.

Making the Strategy Emotionally Relevant

While the specifics differed for each, the other CEOs in our sample told us their own strategic stories in ways that struck many of the same notes. For example, Marjorie Scardino, CEO of Pearson, an international media company, spoke of "creating a company that would be motivating to the people working in it," as well as "looking for a great market, and a business where they could achieve leadership positions around the world."

Anders Dahlvig talked about making the strategy at IKEA "emotionally relevant." What he meant, he explained, "was having some sort of social ambition as part of your business idea . . . Our vision is to create a better range of goods: we want to make sure that people who are on a budget can buy good furniture. It's about design and function at prices low enough to make it possible even for people who are single parents to afford it."

"Of course," Dahlvig noted, "we have to make money on the bottom line; otherwise we couldn't keep running the business." IKEA had to connect the external vision to a set of distinctive internal strengths that could allow it to deliver high-quality design at low prices and still be profitable. "From the very beginning, when we started with the business idea, our entire business model meant that we did things completely differently," he said.

For a company whose trademark is high-quality design, IKEA's key insight was not to start with design, Dahlvig explained: "One of the secrets behind us is that, say, a table doesn't start with a designer making a drawing of something he thinks looks good." Instead, he noted, "there is a product range strategy behind it: What are the prices? What are the quality factors? What is the range expression? So that the finished table will suit the market." He continued, "You need to understand the entire supply process—the materials and where they come from, how they can be used for products, and how the production process compares. We need to understand how the production process works for different kinds of material so that we can calculate what the price tag is going to be for the end-user before actually designing the product."

Doing things differently at IKEA, however, goes far deeper than just having a well-honed, design-to-cost product development process. Dahlvig emphasized: "Our values are different. We encourage discussion. Those are our values, those are the kind of people we pick—people who question things, who like constant change and development. That is a driving force within our culture, within this system." In turn, that culture of open discussion and questioning is nurtured and sustained by a deeper set of values and choices. The soul of IKEA, in Dahlvig's view, "is the way we treat each other in the company, the way we are as human beings. Removing all the barriers between bosses and employees, symbolic and nonsymbolic, working in close proximity to each other. There is a sense of community, an openness between bosses and staff."

These core elements of IKEA's identity were already deeply rooted when Dahlvig took over in 1999. But with IKEA's growth and development, its strategic identity also needed to evolve. In terms similar to a parent describing an adolescent child who is growing up, Dahlvig spoke of IKEA as "having been an entrepreneurial company that had grown out of its clothes. We had to go through the whole process of becoming a major company, to manage being big with all that entails. However, at the same time, we wanted to keep many of the positive features of entrepreneurship."

In the 1970s and 1980s, IKEA went from being a Swedish company to a company with a presence in all of Europe and North America, almost twenty countries in twenty years. In essence, Dahlvig recalls, "it was a strategy of entering a country and opening a few stores, and then we would jump into the next country, instead of penetrating that market more deeply." A consequence of the rapid expansion was that IKEA had become known as a niche player.

Dahlvig and his senior colleagues saw the need to change strategies. Instead of working toward expansion to an ever-growing number of countries, "our strategy would be to broaden our customer base in markets where we were already present and could become market leaders," he remarked.

At first glance, this might seem a modest shift. But Dahlvig explained why it was a fundamental strategic change: "Until then, our profile had shown us being different, a company entering the market with a Swedish or Scandinavian profile, which appealed to a restricted group of customers in Germany or Britain or wherever." People viewed Scandinavian design as something distinct, not directly addressing local mass-market tastes. To deepen IKEA's presence, to become a market leader, "a lot of new things were demanded of us in terms of strategy: how to gain acceptance of our product range by a much broader customer base," he said.

Getting IKEA to make this shift, Dahlvig realized, would require a deeper strategy process than its existing planning approach, one that would entail extensive involvement by people at all levels across the organization. He explained, "We began by creating a plan, which we called, 'Ten Jobs in

Ten Years.' So you could say it was a ten-year plan. We'd never had that before. We had always worked with three-year plans and one-year plans." But three years was too short for the transformation Dahlvig was envisioning.

The ten-year plan, which took about a year to create, "gave direction for our way forward and set various priorities and objectives," Dahlvig said. "It took another year to start implementing it and to ensure it was anchored throughout the organization. You can't provide the answers to all the questions with a ten-year plan; the organization must find solutions within these guidelines and ambitions. We produced action plans with a three-year perspective. And the stores have one-year plans."

As the Nokia and IKEA stories illustrate, developing or recrafting an organization's strategic identity is a deeper process than simply articulating a new strategy. The CEOs of these firms were deeply involved personally in an iterative, intuitive process, paying close attention to their current successes and failures, probing their organization's character and potential sources of advantage, while often putting a wide cross-section of the organization to work on different aspects of developing strategy and ensuring alignment with it. As Ollila described it, "There's a lot of communication, which is very direct, with lots of examples shown of what it means. In the early nineties, even with the difficulties, we had hundreds of people working on our strategy. Later we may have had a thousand or two thousand people. So you build alignment, you build engagement."

Many of the CEOs described how extensively they traveled to engage people at all levels in redirecting the company. They emphasized, however, this was not just to build support, but a genuine opportunity for them to learn about the company and what could prevent or accelerate execution, often leading to further refinements to the strategy. They did not see engaging a cross-section of employees in strategic dialogue as a massive one-off campaign to launch a transformation, but rather as an ongoing process. As Sherrill Hudson, CEO of TECO Energy, observed, "strategy is one of those things you constantly have to upgrade."

The picture the CEOs painted was very different from the rationally focused, often consultant-driven exercise that frequently constitutes strategy making. Instead, informed by a keen understanding of current business performance and learning from their successes and failures, they described a process of deepening insight into where the distinctive people, capabilities, and culture of their enterprise could provide advantage. As these CEOs engaged in real discussion and debate with their people, they forged a shared sense of strategic identity and meaningful purpose, one that would resonate deeply with the organization: making both money and meaning.

See Organizational Capability as Strategy

In defining the strategic transition during his tenure, Dahlvig spoke of IKEA's shift in the marketplace from niche to mass market, and then gave equal or more emphasis to the organizational dimensions of "moving away from being a small player to becoming a big one." He explained why this was so significant: "The individual units until then had been working independently of each other. We had extensive local freedom and a very limited central IKEA staff. We didn't really reap those benefits of scale that spring from being a big company, because everybody was doing their own thing. We wouldn't have been able to grow if we had continued in the same vein."

The opportunity he saw was simultaneously unleashing the entrepreneurialism of the store managers, while also gaining the benefits of scale. That required, in his view, a mental readjustment: "Instead of being national, we were going to become global/local. What we were really doing was eliminating responsibility in the middle, at the level of the country organization, so we could lift up responsibility globally and also pull it in the direction of the local store."

The consequences were far-reaching. The country organizations experienced a major readjustment in terms of power and activities, and ultimately reduced their head counts by 35 percent to 40 percent.

The role of the store manager expanded, with multiple consequences. "It turned out," recalled Dahlvig, "that many store managers didn't live up to expectations. That's why we have increased local accountability. We have set up local boards, something we didn't have before, so that today each store is like a company."

The shift in power to the global functions did not significantly increase the head count at IKEA's central office, as one might have expected. Instead, Dahlvig explained, "when we carry out development projects, it's our principle not to hire permanent staff here at headquarters. Over the project period, we finance a number of people who return to their units on completion of the project. We pay for them while they are here, and they continue under their contract of employment in Germany or China or Russia or wherever." There was a clear rationale behind this approach: "Your knowledge becomes obsolete fairly quickly if you become permanently employed in a dedicated function. That's why we believe it is better to pick people to work with development projects on a temporary basis and send them back into the business afterwards."

Other CEOs were equally focused on the strategic nature of their organizational choices. As we have seen, Peter Sands remarked on how Standard Chartered Bank's ability to make an organizational matrix work with strong country organizations as well as strong global product businesses underpinned its success in being locally responsive yet gaining the benefits of its geographic reach. Volvo's Leif Johansson elaborated at length on how the organization's capacity to consolidate the number of engine platforms was the linchpin of its global truck strategy. In each case, the CEOs highlighted how their organizational strengths enabled them to bring together hard-to-combine characteristics (such as scale and entrepreneurialism, in the case of IKEA) in ways that their competitors could not match. Ollila spoke of the inextricable linkage between strategy and organization at Nokia: "Because the technology was not only a breakthrough in terms of growth potential, but disruptive in the sense that it killed some old stuff, we could actually create an exceptional company—not just a growth company, but an exceptional company." He continued, "We did two things at the same time. We moved from a Finnish base to be a truly global company. And we moved with a breakthrough or disruptive technology."

In retrospect, it is hard to fully appreciate the breathtaking nature of the dual challenge Nokia was taking on. In order to sell to the emerging markets, primarily in Asia, clearly the company would have to invest in building up substantial local organizations, especially in distribution, with people and a mix of cultures very different from its base of Finnish engineers. What's more, devising a "phone for everybody" would require a very different approach to design, manufacturing, and marketing than would the toy for executives. It meant developing a phone that would work for people who live and work in jungles and fields, towns and villages, as well as in cities, suburbs, and office buildings. These considerations had implications for phone size, functionality, reliability, and cost.

The company translated the strategy into a set of guidelines for the product itself. In 1994, Ollila told us, the company defined goals that it called "100 to the power of 4." It said that, within five years, the handset would have to weigh no more than 100 grams, be a maximum of 100 cubic centimeters in size, contain no more than 100 components, and cost no more than $100. "We were setting targets that were way off the scale, that looked really crazy, because phones were really big then," Ollila said. "Yet, in the year 2000, six years later, we had beaten all except one." The one missed target was the number of components, which still hovers around three hundred, although that's half of the six hundred it contained in 1994.

The small, light, simple, and cheap phone proved immensely appealing to people around the world. "Look at our market share in China, India, Latin America, the Middle East, Africa," Ollila said. "The deeper you go into the jungle or into the clay huts in India, the closer it is to 80 percent share." And Ollila, typical of the CEOs in our sample, had gone into the field to see his products at work firsthand: "In a clay hut in India, I asked this guy, 'Why do you have a Nokia phone?' He said, 'This is my second phone. When I bought my first one three years ago, I was told by the dealer that this is the best and I would get the best money out of it when I sell it to the next guy.' And he was right."

Ollila observed that it is easy to have a strategy to be more innovative than your competitors, but much harder to make it happen in practice. Innovative companies face the dilemma of how to achieve focus without heavy-handed control, how to channel innovation without killing it. Ollila talked at length about that challenge: "If you have costs to worry about, and you take an axe to the operation, that's the end of innovation. But then again, if you have no rules, no guidelines, nothing—a lot of companies have been killed by that. Because there's no strategy, no vision, no rules, no connection to reality. That has happened many, many times."

Nokia, therefore, sought to create an atmosphere of what might be called organized chaos. That meant that the company would work on a number of ideas at once, but would focus on those that were advanced and seemed to have big potential as valuable intellectual property, because no one was really sure where the industry was headed. Management had to make decisions, however, about how long to keep pouring resources into any of these nascent ideas. At Nokia (and at other cellphone companies), one of the promising projects was the speech codec, a method for compressing speech for digital transmission. Twenty engineers had worked for three years on Nokia's speech codec, but had little to show for their efforts. The project was finally terminated, and the engineers moved to other projects that seemed more relevant and promising and that needed the help. Nokia went with a speech codec from another company.

A year later, the speech codec had become an even more central technology to mobile telephony, and Ollila began to wonder if Nokia had made the right decision to stop work on its own version. Then he got a call from an R&D manager, "who doesn't really know whether he should be proud or totally embarrassed, saying that we had five guys who had continued the work, without any permission, because they thought that management was a bunch of fools and didn't know what they were doing. They had come in weekends or evening time with no hours counted. And now, it seems, we have the best speech codec in the world. This is what Nokia is all about."

This combination of pride, passion, personal commitment, and loyalty made Nokia a world leader in cell phones and a place where people who care about them wanted to work. "There's a huge pride in the organization," Ollila told us, "which you create with the right kind of guidance, goal setting, motivation, and treating people well—giving the right people a bonus or a promotion or a pat on the back or a bucket of beer on a Friday. It's not about huge money bonuses. It's these small things, as long as they are right, and as long as you praise even bad behavior. I mean bending the rules a bit (as, for example, with the speech codec), as long as it gets results for the company."

Commit, Yet Adapt

The process of defining its strategic identity enabled Nokia and other higher-ambition companies to commit to those parts of the business portfolio that fit and defined a natural trajectory for growth. A number of higher-ambition leaders explicitly capitalized on their companies' distinctive organizational capabilities and approach to pursue strategies as preferred acquirers—for example, Sands at SCB; David Langstaff at U.S. defense company Veridian; and Bertrand Collomb at French building materials maker Lafarge.

Clarity in strategic identity also enabled higher-ambition CEOs to exit those businesses that did not fit. As Ollila bluntly put it, having decided to focus on cell phones, "we needed to get rid of the nongrowth products—the cable, the televisions." Yes, the company had made some attempts to pare its portfolio with the sale of parts of its rubber, paper, and electronics businesses. But many other units remained that did not fit Nokia's new strategic identity, despite their long histories and devoted employees. Ollila did not want to sell at the bottom of the cycle, and he also did not want to create more turmoil and disruption too quickly: "People say, 'Gee, there's a new management!,' and then suddenly you announce that you're selling the cable business." This is not good for loyalty or commitment. Ollila waited until the company had improved its performance to complete the work of paring back. Although Nokia sold its paper company in 1992, it waited until the winter of 1994 to sell its German television manufacturing business and its power unit.

But restructuring is difficult and can strain the fabric of connection and belonging these CEOs seek to develop. The sale or closing of a unit, or even the possibility of such a move, can't be discussed publicly, so employees often learn from reports in the media that their business or group has been sold. Ollila remembered, "People came to me crying, 'Why do you do this to me?' Or they would turn angry and not even look at me. There was huge emotion about it, because they could see that Nokia was going to be a good story, and they wanted to be part of it." But widespread agreement on strategic direction helped legitimize Ollila's choices. Even in the midst of the restructuring, Nokia was one of five companies in Europe to receive special commendation for employee satisfaction.

Volvo's Johansson had to make a particularly painful cut in the company's portfolio. Although many have forgotten (or never knew) about Volvo's provenance—just as Nokia's origins as a producer of paper products and rubber boots have been lost in the mists of time—the company was founded as a subsidiary of SKF, a Swedish ball-bearing manufacturer. SKF developed its vehicle-manufacturing branch to increase demand for its products. Among those was a single-row, deep-groove ball bearing known as the *volvo* bearing (Latin for "I roll"), which gave a name to the new line of business. The SKF Group continues to be a major ball-bearing and lubricant manufacturer.

In 1927, Volvo produced its first car, which sold poorly. It wasn't until it launched its first truck, the Series 1, the following year that Volvo began to take off. Today, the Volvo Group is made up of nine business units, including trucks, buses, construction equipment, and airplane technology. But since 1948, when Volvo cars became the group's leading business for the first time, the automobiles had been the iconic heart of the business.

That's why it was so difficult to sell the car business. Johansson explained, "We realized that if we were to manage passenger cars, and commit so many resources to passenger cars, we wouldn't be able to manage the rest. So we were facing a choice between the rest of the group or continuing with passenger cars."

The problem was based in engineering. In 1998, when Johansson's team did a strategic analysis of the business, they saw that virtually every unit produced its own engines. It was "completely bonkers," Johansson said. "Truck engines and construction equipment engines and Volvo Penta engines go together very well, and the same is true of buses." But the passenger cars needed an entirely different type of engine. Selling the car unit would make it possible to streamline and unify engine manufacturing across the group.

So in 1999, just two years after Johansson became CEO, Volvo sold its car unit to Ford Motor Company for $6.5 billion. "Strategically, it was blindingly correct," said Johansson. From the point of view of the human organization, the sale of the car unit still causes pain. "Emotionally," he said, "I miss cars every single day."

Both at Volvo and Nokia, as well as in many of the other companies in our sample, the bulk of the portfolio restructuring was completed early in the tenure of a new leadership team. In other companies, the ongoing process of adaptation led to redefinitions of what was core later in the leader's tenure. The choice in these cases was arguably more difficult, particularly with businesses very much identified with the leader personally.

Yet, what was striking about these leaders was their ability to combine commitment with a clear-eyed recognition of new strategic realities.

At BUPA, Britain's leading private health insurer, for example, CEO Val Gooding told us about selling off the BUPA hospitals. "If I was just running the business according to my own sentiment, I couldn't possibly do it," she said. "I love that business. I've been to all the hospitals, I've met a lot of the staff, I spent time with them. I love those hospitals."

For leaders who are on the frontlines, such painful decisions can hit very close to home. Gooding told us that when the decision to sell the hospitals was made, the director of human resources of the hospital business approached her. "Do you know what you said when you hired me?" the HR director asked. Gooding said no, she did not remember. "I asked, 'Would you sell this division?' And your answer was, 'Not while I'm chief executive.'"

But things had changed at BUPA and in the health-care sector. Changes in government policy had eroded the benefits of combining insurance and care delivery in a single organization. Increasing opportunities for private contracting meant the hospitals could potentially expand faster if not constrained by an insurance company parent. Faced with the changed economic logic, Gooding reflected, "I'm not really paid to love things, if that's going to distort sensible business decision making."

Beyond decisions about portfolio, the process of forging strategic identity serves to create a powerful internal gyroscope that helps the company maintain strategic consistency and to channel innovation in the right strategic directions.

Dahlvig highlighted the value of stability and sustained commitment: "We've had the same business idea, the same product range for all these years, and simply developed it further. We've invested in communications, brand building, and it hasn't been in vain. We've simply built and built and built." The result, he noted, is that IKEA has the number-one most-recognized retailing brand in the world, despite being ranked as the thirty-fifth largest retailer by sales: "Our stability, combined with our uniqueness and the soft elements in our values—it's those things that have made us more famous than big."

Yet Dahlvig also emphasized that stability needs to be balanced by innovation. "One of our strong points is that we have stability in the big picture and also innovation in the detail. The framework is very stable—the business idea, the concept, the overall plan, the strategies," he said. But, he continued, we are "extremely innovative in the way we develop things over the course of our journey."

Ollila also described how sustained commitment was at the root of Nokia's success, fueling multiyear investments in its distribution networks, in its product platforms, in its brand, and in its technical capabilities. As a result, in 1998, six years after putting cell phones at the center of the company's strategy, Nokia surpassed Motorola to become the world's largest producer of cell phones.

Ollila drew a sharp contrast with Motorola, where there were changing fashions with changing CEOs. "Look at Motorola. It's a story of inconsistency, despite the legacy of fantastic technology. It's a fantastic company with so many good engineers. But it's internal tribes competing with each other, killing each other. And management is giving very mixed signals all the time," he said. The multiple changes in direction, Ollila explained, created "fundamental problems with the software, with the operating system, with operating platform choices. They lost the ball and haven't been able to grab it since."

The higher-ambition CEOs were acutely aware that finding the appropriate balance between committing and adapting is a never-ending challenge. The consistency enabled by a strong strategic identity can become a liability if not refreshed when industry dynamics change, as Nokia's experience illustrates. With nearly two decades of sustained focus, Nokia built and maintained dominant positions in the major developing economies. Yet a strategic orientation that prioritized the mass market left Nokia vulnerable to Apple's high-end breakthrough with the smart phone. Former employees report that Nokia had a prototype handset with a touch-screen and internet compatibility as early as 2004, three years before the launch of the iPhone, but that the company saw it as too expensive to produce and did not pursue it further.[1] The dramatic success of the smart phone forced Nokia onto the defensive, struggling to produce a product that could compete successfully in the most-advanced markets. Yet, even as its market share in the United States trended to low single digits, its continuing strength in the developing markets enabled it to maintain leadership in global smart-phone market share in 2010.[2]

As Johansson put it, it is a mistake to think a company has ever arrived at a finished state: "Companies are never finished. You can never really say, 'now we're done.'"

Conclusion

At the heart of higher ambition is a commitment to building a thriving and enduring human institution. The success of that institution depends on the capabilities and aspirations of the flesh-and-blood human beings who are its members.

In this context, the CEO's role as chief strategist moves from an analytic and numbers-driven exercise to a developmental task, akin to helping individuals come into their own and redefine their identity as they make the transition from one life stage to the next—from childhood to adolescence, from adolescence to adulthood. At each of these stages, people undergo a shift in their sense of who they are, their personal identity, that is deeply rooted in their ability to successfully align passions, capabilities, and values with the opportunities the world provides. Making these transitions can be both liberating and wrenching. Holding on too tightly to a past identity (for example, the successful high school athlete who can't acknowledge that he doesn't have the speed required to make it in the pros) is just as destructive as not understanding one's core strengths.

Analogously, as we have described, our CEOs engaged their people in an interactive process that resulted in a new strategic identity that linked head (a clear-eyed understanding of marketplace opportunities and challenges), hands (a distinctive core of people and capabilities), and heart (values, purpose, and passions). They then built the organizational and business capabilities required to successfully enact this identity. These strategic identities were rooted in current capabilities and embodied a sense of aspirational stretch as to what these firms could become (much as a great mentor or coach builds on and develops an athlete's natural strengths to compete at a higher level). A well developed sense of strategic identity provided a compass for sustained investment that reinforced core strengths. Maintaining this identity, in the context of a changing market required ongoing adaptation and paring away of aspects of the firm that were no longer critical to future success.

By directly involving a wide range of people in strategic dialogues about the firm's direction, while setting high aspirations for both business performance and social value, these leaders increase commitment and boost the energy level. By speaking both to heads and hearts, and demonstrating a willingness to listen and learn from people's points of view concerning strategy, they earn trust, reduce friction, and build the fortitude needed to follow through on difficult choices.

In table 3-1, we contrast the common leadership pattern with the higher-ambition leaders' approach and summarize how, in forging strategic identity, higher-ambition leaders adopt an approach that both includes but also goes a step beyond traditional management best practices.

TABLE 3-1

Forging strategic identity

<table>
<thead>
<tr>
<th></th>
<th colspan="2">HIGHER-AMBITION LEADERS' APPROACH</th>
</tr>
<tr>
<th>Common leadership pattern</th>
<th>Management "best practices"</th>
<th>Additional distinctive practices</th>
</tr>
</thead>
<tbody>
<tr>
<td colspan="3">CRAFT STRATEGIC IDENTITY</td>
</tr>
<tr>
<td>
• The strategy development process is primarily driven by external consultants and internal staff functions

• The strategy is largely based on quantitative analysis
</td>
<td>
• General manager serves as lead strategist

• Compelling strategy leverages sources of competitive advantage

• High-involvement processes used for developing strategy
</td>
<td>
• The strategy development process is intuitive as well as rational and uncovers organizational sources of advantage

• The strategy defines a social purpose and resonates with the firm's heritage and identity

• The strategy development process is as much about gaining alignment around the strategy as it is about developing it
</td>
</tr>
<tr>
<td colspan="3">SEE ORGANIZATIONAL CAPABILITY AS STRATEGY</td>
</tr>
<tr>
<td>
• Strategy and organization are viewed as separate areas of focus

• The source of superior strategy is considered to be superior intellectual insight
</td>
<td>
• Execution is understood as an essential element of strategy

• Organizational capacity is built in order to implement strategy
</td>
<td>
• The strategy capitalizes on distinctive cultural and organizational strengths

• The organizational design creates competitive advantage by bringing together characteristics that are typically hard to combine (e.g., matrix structures with strong geographies but also strong global businesses and functions)
</td>
</tr>
<tr>
<td colspan="3">COMMIT, YET ADAPT</td>
</tr>
<tr>
<td>
• Current performance is paramount

• When management changes, so does strategy
</td>
<td>
• Make bold moves into areas consistent with strategy

• Portfolio is periodically refocused
</td>
<td>
• The business portfolio emphasizes depth and focus rather than broader diversification

• The company invests over many years to develop superior capabilities and high-quality relationships with customers, suppliers, and other key stakeholder groups
</td>
</tr>
</tbody>
</table>

4

Building a Shared Commitment to Excel

People won't get fulfillment from an organization
that isn't recognized as being high performance.

—Brian Walker, Herman Miller

You create an environment that's
self-governing. You can't govern it all.

—Doug Conant, Campbell Soup Company

HAVING A HIGHER AMBITION is one thing, but it's quite another to actually deliver on the promise of creating and sustaining superior economic and social value. To do so requires that leaders throughout the organization commit to raising aspirations and performance expectations. As Tim Solso of Cummins explained, "it is not enough for a company's people to have a 'best efforts' mind-set, in which they say to themselves, 'I'm smart, I work hard, I did everything I could, and that's the best I can do,' as opposed to, 'Did I do what I said I was going to do?'"

Moving to a high-performance culture cannot be mandated. Employees must see it first as legitimate, then ultimately as essential to organizational pride. Ironically, we found that it was precisely companies like Cummins, with a long and distinguished commitment to a larger social purpose, that faced the greatest challenge in creating a high-performance culture. Such companies tended to have "nice" cultures in which managers found directly confronting performance problems difficult. But higher-ambition leaders saw that the failure to set a high performance standard has negative consequences, not just for competitiveness, but also for the commitment of their people. Herman Miller's Brian Walker explained, "People won't get fulfillment from an organization that isn't recognized as being high performance." Steven Holtzman, former CEO of Infinity Pharmaceuticals, suggested that the best employees need colleagues around them who will "raise them up" so that they can do their best work. He remarked that world-class talent attracts world-class talent, not unlike in jazz: "Coltrane wants to play with Parker even though he can succeed elsewhere, right?"

As you may recall from our discussion of Campbell Soup Company in chapter 1, it was hard for anyone to imagine that Campbell could become a magnet for world-class talent when Doug Conant became CEO in 2001. The company did not have the kind of inspiring aspirations that might attract smart, talented people. Employees just hoped that, somehow, their company could avoid a complete rout in the marketplace, escape total disaster in the stock market, and somehow hang on until something positive might happen.

As we saw, Conant rather swiftly settled on an unlikely turnaround strategy that centered on the revival of what many observers considered to be an exhausted product: condensed soup.

Conant did not go at his new strategy in a conventional way. He did not implement a program of cost cutting, top-down control, and draconian actions designed to boost short-term results. Rather, he began by rethinking and renegotiating the expectations for performance that he believed had to be met to achieve the long-term, sustainable creation of financial value.

First, Conant made clear to his board of directors and key investors that rebuilding the business would take time. "I was just unwilling to commit to a quick fix," Conant told us. "We wanted to go from being uncompetitive to being competitive in a mature industry where there is well-developed mature competition. It was going to take us three years at least." Conant explained to the board that standards and discipline had slipped in virtually every area of the company's operations. "We had to get our product quality up to the right standards. We had to restore our consumer spending in the business. We had to manage our price gaps smartly. We had to build our innovation pipelines. And we had to rebuild the infrastructure to support all this work," he said.

Faced with such a dire diagnosis, Campbell's directors might well have considered other options for the beleaguered company, but they supported Conant in his ambition to get Campbell into "fighting form for the long term." What's more, the major investors, members of the founding Campbell family, were eager to restore the company's former luster and to build a business that would be "sustainably good." However, Conant knew that, even with this high-level support, he and the company would have to perform: "I wouldn't want to be sitting in this seat not performing," he remarked.

Knowing that he had a high-level mandate to rebuild the company, Conant turned his attention to his leadership team and worked to align them around the Campbell Success Model, a simple articulation of what would be required to create and sustain long-term value. As we learned in chapter 1, it had two components: "winning in the marketplace" and "winning in the workplace." To ensure that the model would be more than just words, Conant established simple, clear performance metrics for each. Winning in the marketplace would be measured by total shareholder returns relative to peer companies. Winning in the workplace would be evaluated by levels of employee engagement as measured by the Gallup Employee Engagement Index.

Conant was relentless in driving for higher performance on both metrics. "Of the 505 leaders at Campbell who were originally surveyed, over 270 were in Gallup's bottom quartile," Conant recalled. At the time of our conversation with Conant, the number of leaders in the bottom category had dropped from 270 to 38. "You declare yourself and you systematically work to do better, making the tough calls in a timely and tender way when you have to," he said. He brought this same level of discipline to winning in the marketplace. "Every year we measure our total share-owner returns relative to our peer group," Conant told us. "Our goal is to have, over a decade, the best total share-owner returns in our industry. All the math we've done says that if we can stay above average on a rolling three-year basis over that decade, we will be the best. Inevitably, people reach too high and fall down. In a world that demands excellence every quarter, you've got to be consistently above average."

Declaring a new set of measurements does not mean that everyone accepts or supports them. Conant soon realized that he was meeting at least as much resistance to these performance aspirations from his internal leadership team as he had experienced from the financial analysts to his declaration that condensed soup would save the company. "One of the key challenges we encountered early on was that the organization had a scarcity mentality," Conant said. "It was, 'Well, what do you want us to do? Do you want us to deliver this year? Or do you want us to set the table for next year?' We've had to drive hard to build an abundance mentality. Which is: we're going to do both. We have to win in the marketplace, and we have to win in the workplace, too. It's easier to get to one or the other. It's harder to do both. But if you want to be extraordinary, you have to do both."

To overcome the resistance, Conant devoted a great deal of attention to establishing the legitimacy of his performance expectations. He realized that he couldn't expect others to live up to the new performance expectations unless he and his executive team lived up to their promises to them. "We had the Campbell's Promise, which grew out of a comment I made the first day of work. I said, 'We can't expect you to value our agenda as an executive team until we tangibly demonstrate to you that we value your agenda. In my experience, it doesn't work any other way.'" The Campbell's Promise essentially says that the company values its people and their personal aspirations. When people come to believe that is true, they are inspired to value the Campbell corporate agenda as well.

To make the promise real, Conant developed criteria for evaluating leadership performance, which became known as the Campbell leadership model. As Conant explained: "The Campbell leadership model said the first expectation we have of you is to inspire trust. You have to earn the right to lead. The second thing is you have to create direction in collaboration with your teammates. The third thing is you have to align the organization to execute on that direction. The fourth thing we said is that, once you've got the direction clear and aligned, then you have to build organization vitality—motivate and inspire the people to go do it. The fifth thing is to execute the plan with excellence. The sixth is to produce extraordinary results. Anything we were working on had to connect to the mission to be extraordinary."

Conant also realized that earning the right to lead began with him. He explained:

How do you win over the organization? You declare yourself. You do what you say you are going to do. And then you have to make sure you *tell* them you did it, because they're not always paying attention. You have to do this hundreds of times. You build up the emotional bank account. You start out way in the red. You get to neutral. And eventually you get to the place where you're in the black. I also found early on that to gain the trust of people, I had to eat humble pie when it was appropriate and acknowledge we made some bad decisions. I made some bad hires that I had to deal with earnestly and clearly and say, you know, I made a mistake—and then move on.

Conant's willingness to be held accountable enabled him to build a culture in which managers felt accountable for delivering on their promises, not just to Conant, but to each other. "You have to start forcing executives to share with one another. You create an environment that's self-governing. You can't govern it all," he said.

To build this sense of shared accountability, Conant made a contract with each of his staff members. It stated each person's annual objective and what he or she would do each quarter to deliver on the annual goal. Then each had to do a weekly posting to show how he or she was doing. These were distributed to all the executives on Friday afternoon to read over the weekend. Conant remarked, "We had a staff meeting every Monday, and we talked about how we're doing. Every executive had an opportunity to ask questions. It quickly became a process that was self-governing. When a staff member would present at the Monday meeting a result that did not meet expectations, he might say, 'Yeah, but it's going to be better next week.' One of the executives around the table would say, 'Didn't you say last week that it was going to be better this week?'"

Conant's approach to building a different performance management culture and to making that culture real—both through his personal actions and through a disciplined set of operating processes—paid off, both in the workplace and in the marketplace. Campbell's Gallup results have improved dramatically. It ranked in the ninth percentile in 2001; in 2009, the company had climbed to the eighty-second percentile for overall employee engagement. And from its 2001 employee engagement ratio of 1:1, in 2009, the company achieved a world-class engagement ratio of 23:1 among all employees, and 77:1 in its top 350. At the same time, the company won two awards recognizing its commitment to gender diversity and, in 2010, received a top ranking on a list of socially responsible corporations.[1]

Conant also achieved his goal of above-average performance on a three-year rolling basis. In 2008, Campbell's earnings from continuing operations rose by 7 percent. Even as the economy tanked in 2008, Conant increased ad spending, boosted production, and began construction on a new headquarters building. In September 2008, as Lehman Brothers filed for bankruptcy and financial markets ground to a halt, the share price of 499 of the companies in the S&P 500 dropped. Campbell was the only one that didn't.

As Conant's story illustrates, the leaders in our sample have a higher ambition for how they manage performance: to build a worthy institution that delivers superior results quarter after quarter, and year after year. To ensure that their organizations arc able to deliver on this promise of sustained high performance, higher-ambition leaders:

- Create a culture of accountability.

- Earn the right to lead.

- Build the future one quarter at a time.

- Focus on the fundamentals that drive sustainable success.

Crcate a Culture of Accountability

At the core of establishing a performance management discipline is a simple moral precept—deliver on your promises. We have seen how Conant increased transparency and peer-to-peer accountability in his weekly staff meetings to build an ethic of increased performance accountability for delivering on commitments.

Peter Sands and the leadership team at Standard Chartered Bank helped build a performance ethic by bringing in the voice of investors. SCB was a company with a lot of promise that treated its people well and had a strong sense of ethics, but it had not delivered on its performance commitments. As Sands explained, although the bank was operating in some of the fastest-growing parts of the world, it had largely failed to realize the potential of those markets, thus earning itself the "jam tomorrow" epithet. "We said, 'You've got to hear what these people outside are saying, because it's not pretty,'" Sands recalled. "The conversations we had with investors in the first two months were brutal." While preparing the budget for 2003, for example, the head of consumer banking, Mike DeNoma, set up a conference call with a hundred bank managers and three outside analysts. "He did that as his way of setting up the discussion around what the target should be, and the shape of it, and how they should think about it," Sands said. "And he wasn't saying they're necessarily right; he just said, 'You've got to understand. If you're interested in shareholder value, this is what's going on out there.'" This dose of external reality helped to realign SCB's people on the need to drive for higher performance. As Sands explained, they actually "loved it. They said, 'why hasn't anybody told us before?'"

Unfortunately, some of the leaders in our sample had a much more difficult time convincing their people of the need to improve their performance ethic. We encountered the most dramatic example of the challenge of shifting performance standards at Mahindra & Mahindra.

K. C. Mahindra and his brother J. C., along with partner Ghulam Mohammed, founded Mahindra & Mahindra (M&M) in 1945 to assemble Jeeps in a franchise arrangement with Willys Corp., the U.S. manufacturer of the four-wheel-drive vehicles. Anand Mahindra is the grandson of J. C.; his uncle is Keshub Mahindra, the company's chairman. Anand received his MBA from Harvard Business School in 1981. At the time, the Indian economy was growing, and Anand's father beckoned him back to India to join the family business. Anand decided that the opportunity looked bright and joined Mahindra Ugine, M&M's steel business, as executive assistant to the director of finance. The timing proved unfortunate. "The moment I came," Mahindra told us, "the economy tanked." In an attempt to provide it with a shot in the arm, India then deregulated the steel industry, and as the country fell deeper and deeper into recession, thirty-three new competitors sprang up. Mahindra had little to do because the business itself had little to do. In addition, he didn't find it easy being the son of one of the owners who had just arrived from the United States, especially with the rather nepotistic sounding title of executive assistant. "Everybody had suspicions and would push me aside," Mahindra said. Finally, however, things got so bad that everybody realized the company could not continue in its sleepy ways. That's when they asked, "Where's that MBA?" They charged Mahindra with turning the company around, which, over the next ten years, he successfully did.

During his years at the steel business, Mahindra had resisted a number of overtures from the company's directors, who wanted him to join the auto business. "Why don't you shift and join your uncle's company?" they would say. "There are no heirs here. Why don't you come in? You have the credentials." But Mahindra would reply that he still had work to do at the steel business. In 1991, however, in the wake of a failed takeover attempt, the pressure on him mounted. The economy was on the skids again. M&M had suffered its first-ever operating loss.

Mahindra finally agreed to join the auto unit. There, he found a stagnant environment, not unlike the steel business when he had joined it a decade earlier. "This was a company that had for years been dormant because it had a license to produce Jeeps," Mahindra said. "It never had competition." Once again, in response to the economic crisis, India opened up still further, liberalizing whole industries and allowing in substantially greater amounts of foreign investment. "All of a sudden, you are looking at a future that was going to be potentially flooded—inundated—with competition, both locally and abroad," Mahindra said. "There are people saying, 'You're not going to last more than a couple of years. You better get out of the auto business.'"

The critics were right that Mahindra & Mahindra was in no condition to compete on the world stage. "Productivity was abysmal," Mahindra said.

"Work discipline and quality were abysmal." This was largely because of India's labor laws, which made it almost impossible to increase production or improve productivity. As reported in a 1993 article in the *Globe and Mail,* "Every time Mahindra increases production, it must increase its labor force. As a result, says deputy managing director Anand Mahindra, assembly-line employees work an average of 3.5 hours a day, which makes his unit labor cost only slightly lower than those for a car manufacturer in the United States. In 1992, Mahindra imposed a new rule: no card-playing on the factory floor. No matter, he says. Idle employees lie down beside the assembly line and sleep."[2]

This unproductive state of affairs cannot be attributed only to Mahindra or its management; the social and economic environment also played a role. M&M had been protected for so many years, it had not had to worry much about many of the standard challenges that most for-profit companies face. "When you have a monopolistic environment, why on earth would you invest in R&D, invest in technology?" Mahindra asked. "The people who ran the company were the manufacturing guys, because they were the only ones who determined profit and output. The selling was not a problem, since there was very little competition. Quality was never an issue that you worried about. So you never needed general management strategies of any kind."

Mahindra was also aware that M&M had a number of real strengths. There was an "incredible we're-all-in-this-together mentality," Mahindra told us. "There's a real feeling that, when our backs are to the wall, don't mess with M&M. I inherited that." Mahindra also found a set of ethical values that manifested itself most strongly in a way that we thought a bit surprising: internal auditing. "If you ask me which was the best damn department here, it was internal audit," he told us. "There was a very strong internal audit culture."

But, of course, even world-class auditing is not a generative process; a company needs to conduct revenue-producing activities that are worth auditing. Mahindra decided that, since manufacturing drove the business, the company would have to begin its transformation on the shop floor. As he toured the main engine plant, stepping over sleeping workers as he went, he realized that "this is where we need to make the change first." He engaged a consultancy with experience in auto manufacturing to help M&M with business process reengineering, with the goal of reducing costs and increasing productivity, while still adhering to the labor laws.

But Mahindra could not accept the lack of performance and realized that he would have to build a different level of performance ethic on the shop floor. He chose to announce this just before Diwali, the Indian festival of lights, celebrated in September or October, when M&M distributed the annual bonus to its workers. "*Bonus* sounds like a bonus you give for performance," Mahindra said. But it was obvious that bonuses at the M&M plant "had nothing to do with performance. It had just become an entitlement."

Mahindra spoke to the factory employees at the main engine plant. He told them the company was not doing very well financially, that competition was only going to get tougher, and that, in return for the annual bonus, he expected employees to give something, perhaps something as simple and indicative of a new approach to performance as *not sleeping on the factory floor*. Although he did not directly threaten to withhold bonuses, his message still did not go over well. Diwali is an important holiday, and emotions were already running high at the plant. People counted on their bonuses to shop for food and gifts, and were making plans to celebrate with their families.

A little while after he had made his announcement to the employees, Mahindra looked out his window and saw that workmen were abandoning their stations on the factory floor, banding together, and rushing toward his office. "I remember them running towards me and saying, 'There's the boss! Let's get him!' They were a pretty wild mob," Mahindra said. Fortunately, four union leaders were there and realized what might happen.

They shoved Mahindra into a back room, stepped inside with him, and locked the door. "If I had been out there," Mahindra said, "I would have been thrown over the balcony. They were that emotional. I was under siege. They were banging at the door. I actually called my wife and told her, 'I may not make it back.'"

After four hours, the employees calmed down, and Mahindra decided to go out and talk with them. The union leaders advised him not to, but he went ahead. "I walked out and I said, 'Sit down.' They all sat down. I said, 'Look, I'm here. You want to throw me over this balcony? You can do it. But that won't change anything. The world is changing, and there's not going to be a free lunch anymore. If you want to throw me off now, fine. You want to talk? I'll come back tomorrow and talk.'" When he was finished, the workers' self-appointed leader agreed to meet the next day, after which the workers came up and shook Mahindra's hand. "One of them even asked for my autograph," he said.

In retrospect, Mahindra realized that he had not chosen the best time to renegotiate performance expectations. "Diwali's like Christmas. You don't negotiate and tell people after fifty years to give up something at Christmas time. And they were about to go shopping and so on. To be honest, I underestimated," he told us. But Mahindra had also established his legitimacy as a leader. He made it clear that the demands for higher performance were not arbitrary, but linked to the reality of a newly competitive marketplace. And his insistence on a higher level of performance paid off. Now, said Mahindra, "our productivity is second to none."

Earn the Right to Lead

A critical reason the leaders in our sample were able to establish a higher performance standard for their people was that they set an equally high standard for themselves. These leaders were well aware, like Conant, that they had to "earn the right to lead."

For example, when Ed Ludwig was promoted from CFO to CEO of Becton Dickinson (BD) in May 1999, he quickly discovered that "we weren't going to make our numbers for the year." The problem was that BD had expanded too much and too quickly in the late 1990s, had let its cost base grow too rapidly, and had completed a number of acquisitions that hadn't fully delivered their expected value. Rather than point the finger at others in the company, however, Ludwig began by doing, in effect, a 360-degree performance assessment of BD's senior leadership, including himself. Early in 2000, he commissioned a task force of sixteen of his best managers to interview key leaders throughout the organization. Their goal was to identify the issues that were standing in the way of BD's success, by which Ludwig meant the creation of both financial and social value for the long term. BD is, after all, a company whose vision is to be as well known for its contributions to global health as the Red Cross is.

After the task force had completed its work, the members identified two main barriers to success. The first was a project called Genesis, a multimillion-dollar implementation of an SAP software solutions system, that Ludwig had been leading as CFO. He had intended Genesis to be a way to deal with manufacturing issues and the IT problems associated with Y2K, and had expanded it into other areas of the business. By the time Ludwig became CEO, Genesis "was really off track," he said. The design wasn't working right. This implementation group had isolated itself from others. A hundred million dollars had been spent, and the project was far from complete. What's more, as Ludwig put it, "my name was all over it."

The second issue was that BD offered its distributors incentive programs that tended to distort their ordering patterns, thereby causing significant supply chain inefficiencies. While these types of incentive programs were common in the industry at the time, they were inconsistent with Ludwig's aspiration to manage the company for the long term. Ludwig responded to the findings of the employee task force by taking personal responsibility for fixing both of these problems. He stood up before his senior leadership team and the members of the task force and said, "These things are wrong. One is broken and the other isn't the right answer for us or our distributors, and we're going to stop." He promised that BD would "stop offering these distributor incentives by the end of the year, even if it means missing our numbers," and that he was stopping "further implementation of the Genesis project until the problems with it had been fixed."

To make good on these promises, Ludwig had to endure the toughest period in his professional career. He told us that, after the September Labor Day break, "we came out, and said, 'We're restructuring the company.' We took a big charge. We eliminated twelve hundred positions. We terminated the distributor incentive programs, all at the same time. So this was sort of a nuclear blast." From a share price that had reached a high of over $40 at the time of his appointment as CEO, BD's stock fell to a low, below $22 on September 26, 2000.

Then came the breakthrough. Around 7:00 p.m. one evening, the investor relations director burst into Ludwig's office and announced that Rick Wise, an independent investment analyst, had changed his negative view on BD stock and given it a buy rating. "I didn't know Rick Wise from Aunt Tillie," Ludwig told us. "But he said, 'I think Becton Dickinson has gotten religion. They faced the brutal facts.' We almost cried!" By the end of October, BD's share price had rebounded to the mid-$30s.

"That was kind of the end of the beginning," Ludwig said. "What happened after that? We implemented what we said we were going to do." Ludwig delayed implementation of Genesis for a year, at a cost of about $15 million, in order to fix it, but the results proved worth the expense and effort. "We got it right," Ludwig said. He told us that an independent analyst has cited the installation "as one of the most ambitious installations of SAP that they've experienced. People are coming here to learn from us how we do this stuff." And not only did BD end the inefficient distributor incentive programs, it completely revamped its sales and distribution procedures. "Our supply chain now is just unbelievable," Ludwig said. "Order fill rates, efficiencies, back orders—any way you want to measure, it's much better." Gross profit climbed from 48 percent to 52 percent, "and a lot of that is in the supply chain efficiencies," he said.

What about that most conventional metric of financial performance, share price? Ludwig made reference to the analyst, Wise, who, since issuing the buy order, "has made a lot of money for shareholders."

However, perhaps most important for Ludwig was the "trust and credibility" that he gained, he said, "from my team, first of all, and from the rest of the organization, when I stood up and said these things are wrong." The example that Ludwig set enabled him to create a very different performance ethic within the company. He could now ask for the same level of openness and honesty from his organization that he had demonstrated in his own behavior. He explained, "The reason the last six years have been so successful is because we've been brutally honest with ourselves. If you have a $6 billion operation, operating in fifty countries with twenty-seven thousand people, somebody's going to be off their game. What's happened over the last couple years is that the country leaders, the regional leaders, the general managers, and the business presidents are doing a better job anticipating those problems, confronting them, and dealing with them as relatively small problems rather than having them get to be big problems."

Build the Future One Quarter at a Time

Higher-ambition leaders approached the relationship between delivering short-term performance and building the capabilities and assets required for the longer term quite differently than their more traditional peers. Leaders like Conant realized that they were not immune from the pressures of financial markets or boards of directors. However, they also were extraordinarily skillful in managing short-term demands in a way that contributed to the development of long-term capabilities and value. This required working hard to set the right expectations with their boards and investors. Like Conant, these leaders "were unwilling to commit to the quick fix." However, it also required setting expectations with down-the-line leaders so they understood they had to adopt an "abundance mentality," as Conant put it, in which they both "deliver this year," while "setting the table for next year."

This insistence on building the future one quarter at a time led many higher-ambition leaders to focus on driving steady and consistent progress. At Campbell, Conant referred to this as delivering performance that was "consistently above average." As we've seen, his intention was to achieve the best total shareholder returns in his industry over the period of a decade by consistently staying above average on a rolling three-year basis.

Paul Bulcke, CEO of Nestlé, made a similar point about the value of delivering consistent performance in a way that builds long-term success: "The Nestlé model is delivering results year after year. That relates to the question of sustainability, which we define as 5 percent to 6 percent organic growth." (Financial analysts, of course, would like more—7 percent to 8 percent annual growth.) "But if you want to grow healthily, you cannot overgrow in one year. It's not good for your bones, he said. "If you have kids, you know that, too. At a certain age, their arms are too long, and they are clumsy, because they're growing too fast. They're fragile, because the bones are not set. A company like ours, we have to grow healthily. Healthy is what you can absorb. You have to have the human structure and the cohesion in your company. You have to maintain that balance. We are more about balanced long-term growth, rather than maximizing short-term growth." As a result, Bulcke told us, "some analysts may say, 'Come on, Nestlé, you're a little bit boring.'"

The steady cumulative approach these leaders took to driving enhanced performance was strongly related to their aspirations to build worthy and enduring enterprises. As Bulcke suggests, a healthy business, like a healthy child, develops steadily and organically. Too rapid or erratic growth puts the organization at risk of outrunning its capabilities, which, in turn, can lead to all kinds of unhealthy decisions, such as making hasty hires or ill-considered acquisitions. If the bones "don't set right," a business contraction is likely to follow the boom. Then the need for short-term survival can lead to further unhealthy actions, such as staff reductions and the slashing of long-term investments. This is exactly the circle of doom that Conant worked so hard to escape at Campbell. While Bulcke may joke that steady, long-term performance improvement is boring to analysts, it also increases chances that the company will meet market expectations, not just now, but consistently over time.

In addition, a steady cumulative performance trajectory creates the opportunity for ongoing learning, what Conant described as a "continuous improvement" rather than a "quick-fix" approach to building a great company. "It's this whole concept of sustainably good," Conant said. "We are always looking to do a little better this year than we did last year. What's working? What's not? What's needed? What are we going to do better next time?"

Val Gooding, former CEO of BUPA, made a similar point. BUPA tracks the satisfaction and loyalty of both customers and frontline employees. "Our philosophy," she said, "is that the bar must always be higher. Even if it's only a point higher, the target must be higher than what we achieved last year."

Focus on the Fundamentals That Drive Sustainable Success

One of the most powerful ways that higher-ambition leaders created quarter-by-quarter accountability for long-term success was through the metrics they used to assess performance, as well as through how they approached the business review process.

It has become fashionable to deploy multidimensional "balanced scorecards" to assess performance. In our experience, the outcome of these assessments is, in too many cases, not so much balanced as a welter of confusing, disconnected measures. Each functional department lobbies for its metrics to be part of the scorecard, and line managers wonder where they should be focusing their efforts. In the end, the large number of metrics cancel each other out, and the performance management process defaults back to focus on meeting short-term, bottom-line results.

In contrast, the leaders we interviewed tied the performance management process to clear, coherent models for how the business would achieve sustainable success. These models created a strong and balanced accountability for investment in building a great organization, as well as for delivering financial results. Conant built this performance model around two powerful imperatives, each with a simple and clear metric: winning in the marketplace, as measured by total return to shareholders, and winning in the workplace, as assessed by the Gallup Employee Engagement Index results.

Nordea's Christian Clausen provides another good illustration of the systematic and fact-based approaches the leaders take to identifying the drivers of long-term performance and to creating accountability for them. As a first step in measuring performance, Clausen subdivided the bank into a hundred different groups and then compared the ten best-performing ones with the ten poorest-performing ones. What's most interesting is that company leadership conducted the assessment in terms of culture. They identified nine cultural elements they considered to be "good" or "not good." They found that the ten groups that got the highest score for these cultural elements also had the highest scores in all other respects, including financial results. "It was quite unambiguous," Clausen told us. The ten groups that scored highest on the cultural factors had a growth rate of 73 percent. The ten groups that scored lowest on the cultural measures had a 9 percent growth rate. The top scorers had a cost-income ratio of 42 in comparison to the others, which had a ratio of 59. The top groups showed better scores for customer satisfaction, better employment satisfaction, and more. Nordea called this "cultural mapping," and it shared the map with the manager of each group. Clausen explained, "We say, 'This is your cultural mapping—here you see the average, here you see the best.' Everyone could see where the differences were, not just financially, but also in terms of culture. I could see that in terms of customer orientation, I'm here and the best ones are up here."

Our leaders also found that achieving shared insight into key business drivers required a different approach to business planning and review. We were struck by the extent to which our leaders shifted these business planning discussions from a simple negotiation about the numbers to a more in-depth, searching conversation about underlying assumptions and strategy. For example, Dale Morrison explained that, in the past at McCain Foods, the planning process just involved "getting somebody to sell whatever number you wanted to sell—top-line, bottom-line, and stuff in between. But nothing was underpinned, so we shifted the orientation. The numbers now fall out of a plan. If you don't have a plan, you're not running the business the way it should be running. And so, we have a template that we've created to really force out the things the managers should be thinking about as part of the development of a good plan." The result of this planning process was a definition of the three or four important things that the managers were going to do that would have a meaningful impact on the business. "We're in the third year of this approach," Morrison said. "Each year, it's getting better, but it was surprising how at first it was like a foreign language."

Brian Walker described a similar challenge in reeducating people at Herman Miller, a U.S. furniture designer and manufacturer, to understand that the most important part of a good planning process was shared business insight:

> When I work with new product teams, I keep saying, "You guys think a
> business plan is about giving me a document so I'll approve your

program. The business plan isn't for me, it's for you. This should be you painting a picture for yourself about what you're trying to accomplish with this new product. Whether that's what market share you want to get, what problems you're going to try to solve for customers, how big you think it's going to be, what kind of price points you need to get to. It isn't about you knowing all the answers and having them be right. It's about spending the time to sit down and envision for yourselves what you want to be. That will guide you to that spot over time."

Entrenched behaviors are difficult to change. Walker's people argued that, despite what he said about the plans being for their benefit, he would still expect them to be right. "I said, 'No, what I expect is that, when it turns out that your vision isn't happening, you think what you're going to do about it. Are you proactively recognizing when you're off course? Do you know the impact of adjusting course? Rather than assuming that it doesn't matter that you're off, it does matter that you're off, but only in the sense that it helps you guide yourself to a new spot,'" he told us.

Conclusion

Managing performance is central to the work of any CEO. There are few large commercial enterprises in which the annual negotiation of financial targets and regular assessments of performance against plan don't provide a central rhythm and focus of activity. To achieve a higher ambition, leaders have to get the management fundamentals of good performance management right—setting clear goals, ensuring regular and focused reviews, and creating accountability for results achieved.

However, they also have to successfully address a tougher set of challenges. (See table 4-1 for a summary of how higher-ambition leaders both incorporate the disciplines of good performance management and take things a step beyond.) They shift the mind-set of investors and employees in terms of what good performance looks like, from just making the numbers to building a worthy institution that delivers long-term sustainable performance. They do not just set expectations top-down. Instead, they build a collective commitment to high performance. They spend as much time shaping minds (challenging managers to think deeply about the most critical drivers of long-term performance) and hearts (establishing the legitimacy of their performance aspirations through their own actions as well as by linking them to a shared purpose), as they do on refining the mechanics of their performance management processes.

In the previous two chapters, we have seen how higher-ambition leaders create and legitimize powerful new strategic identities and challenging performance aspirations for their enterprises. In the next chapter, we will show how successfully executing on these strategies and delivering on these performance aspirations require building a distinctive set of cultural strengths.

TABLE 4-1

Building a shared commitment to excel

Common leadership pattern	HIGHER-AMBITION LEADERS' APPROACH	
	Management "best practices"	Additional distinctive practices
CREATE A CULTURE OF ACCOUNTABILITY		
• Management approach does not strongly differentiate between high- and low-performing businesses or individuals (e.g., business gets capital primarily based on size; personnel cuts happen across the board)	• A high standard is set and upheld for individual and business performance	• Performance standards are linked to shared aspirations and collective purpose • People feel accountable to peers and themselves to achieve stretch performance standards
EARN THE RIGHT TO LEAD		
• Frustrations with leader's performance and actions only discussed behind closed doors	• Leader actively models commitment to deliver on promises to organization and shareholders	• Leader accepts public accountability for his or her own performance
BUILD THE FUTURE ONE QUARTER AT A TIME		
• Leadership insists on meeting monthly or quarterly targets even at expense of the long term	• Long-term investments are protected despite short-term pressures • Leadership builds a culture of continuous performance improvement	• Short-term requirements are met in ways that build long-term capabilities • Equal discipline and accountability are maintained around short- *and* long-term goals
FOCUS ON THE FUNDAMENTALS THAT DRIVE SUSTAINABLE SUCCESS		
• Business planning focuses primarily on negotiating numbers • Performance reviews typically backward-looking, not learning-focused • "Balanced scorecards" filled with a welter of only loosely connected functional metrics	• Planning process is used to create alignment between strategy, budget, and operating plan • There is strong focus on translating the long-term vision and strategy into key business drivers	• Business performance reviews are based on high levels of open, direct, two-way communication and problem solving • Business reviews used as source of ongoing strategic learning • Clear linkages between business and organizational metrics

5

Creating Community
Out of Diversity

If you thrive on diversity, if you like different foods, if you like to travel, and if you like to speak the global language of bad English, come to us, because that's what we are about.

—Leif Johansson, Volvo

HIGHER-AMBITION LEADERS PLACE great emphasis on developing their organizations as global communities—social organizations that create a mutual sense of belonging that transcends business and functional differences, as well as professional, ethnic, cultural, and national identities. Why do they do so? Because these CEOs have learned that creating a strong social fabric is fundamental to the health of the enterprise and to its financial success. The threads of this fabric—informal relationships across geographies and functions—make collaborating worldwide far easier. As we saw at Standard Chartered Bank, building a genuine sense of community bred personal commitment, created the energy for achieving aspirational goals, and enabled more effective collaboration, in this case, along trade corridors and between the global lines of business and countries.

That corporations can become strong social institutions is hardly a new idea. We have long known that employees' commitment to the organization and to each other can lead to improved performance and well-being in the workplace. But we discovered that the CEOs in our sample were actively reinventing the nature of community. In an earlier form of corporate community based on similarity, employees often lived relatively close to one another, went to the same places of worship, celebrated the same traditions, spoke the same language, saw each other regularly, and often socialized together. In contrast, these CEOs were shaping community out of diversity, finding ways to build a shared purpose and culture within an increasingly globalized enterprise and to integrate the contributions of increasingly specialized and differentiated types of workers and expertise.

In this chapter, we will explore the experience of Tim Solso at Cummins to illustrate the way that community is being reinvented in many of these companies and will highlight the key aspects of how higher-ambition leaders go about building community out of diversity.

"A Shot Heard Round the World"

When Solso took over as CEO of Cummins in 2000, he was inheriting a company whose sense of community had always been one of its great strengths, but defined in a very restricted way. In 1939, Clessie Cummins, the mechanical genius who helped found the company, stated its purpose very simply: it was created to serve the needs of Columbus, Indiana, a small town forty-six miles south of Indianapolis. The company was so rooted in its hometown, and had been for so long, that employees around the world often referred to the Columbus headquarters as Mecca.

The company's business mission was equally well defined: the Cummins Engine Company, Inc., was put on earth to build engines. That was still the mission when Solso became CEO. The company's name, however, was a relic; it did not reflect the scope of Cummins's activities. Thanks to a series of acquisitions and ventures around the world, Cummins was involved in many businesses, including power generation, components, and distribution, along with its original business of diesel engines.

Nor did the focus on Columbus reflect the company's global presence. It had long been international in scope. Its first overseas plant was built in Scotland in 1956; it entered India in 1962 and established its business in China in 1981. When Solso became CEO, the company was operating in thirteen countries with over five hundred sales and service branches worldwide. About 39 percent of the company's sales came from outside the United States.

Solso had been with Cummins for thirty years and might have continued the traditions in which he was thoroughly steeped. To his credit, Solso came into his new job knowing that the company needed transformation. For three decades, Cummins had been struggling to maintain its position as the leading supplier of diesel engines. The trucking industry, Cummins's major market, has always been volatile, so much so that truck equipment sales are considered a leading indicator of the health of the whole U.S. economy. Truck sales drop at the earliest signs of an economic slump, before the sales of other industrial and consumer goods, and pick up again at the first indication that the economy is improving. Partly as a result of this volatility, along with the capital-intensive nature of the business, Cummins had long lived a life of financial instability.

Still, Cummins might have been able to muddle through, and Solso might not have been spurred to act as he did, had the economy held strong. But, by the middle of 2000, the value of the heavy truck market dropped by some 70 percent. Around the same time, many of Cummins's other markets faltered; as Solso put it, "everything went into the tank." Cummins's overextended financials (it had made an acquisition in 1998) put it in a precarious position to weather the storm. Worse, the company had been too optimistic in its forecasts and now found itself with two years of inventory it couldn't sell. Then, its accountancy, Arthur Andersen, came under scrutiny and went out of business in the wake of the Enron blow-up. Andersen's replacement, PricewaterhouseCoopers, found some accounting inconsistencies in two of the company's plants and required Cummins to restate its earnings for the three previous years. This led to an action by the SEC known as a comment letter, which prohibited Cummins from raising money on the capital markets, further weakening its financial position.

What did Solso do? Did he close plants, slash costs, trim the portfolio, and take other drastic measures to shore up the balance sheet? Yes, he did (more on that later). But he knew that he also had to attend to Cummins, the social institution, and that he had to do so immediately. There could be no sequential action here; he needed a simultaneous solve.

Solso knew the social organization needed repair because he saw that there was very little alignment among Cummins leaders on any of the key guiding principles—vision, mission, or values. What's more, there was virtually no corporate strategy. "The way we had done corporate strategy in the past was that a very few people would sit in a closet and come out and say 'Here is a strategy.' And it would change fairly frequently," he told us.

So, in the early months of his tenure, Solso sought to define those crucial missing elements.

First, he began to open up the "inner circle" of people who had been running Cummins—the insiders who had always gotten an invitation into the strategy-making closet. "People who grew up in the engine business in Columbus tended to run the company," Solso said. He built a new group of senior leaders, with members from constituencies beyond the engine business. Most of them had had some kind of international experience. Most important to Solso, "all of them were fed up with the inconsistent results that we had."

Then Solso reached out much more expansively, through a series of focus groups and other activities, to Cummins people around the world.

"We involved thousands of people. They talked about what our vision, mission, and values should be. You'd have twenty people from, let's say, India and say to them, 'OK, half of you please tell us what you think the values of the corporation have been in the past. The other half please tell us the values into the future.'" They gathered all the data, analyzed it and synthesized it, and came up with a new statement of vision, mission, and values. "It wasn't just my interpretation of the values," Solso said, "or the operating committee's interpretation of the values." It was the community's interpretation.

From this process, the new articulation of the company's purpose emerged: "Making people's lives better by unleashing the power of Cummins." Rather than just making engines, "what that meant is what we do is important to *people,*" said Solso. "Unleashing the power" certainly referred to the Cummins business activity, but, more than that, it was about "the innovation of our people. That vision wouldn't mean anything to anybody who didn't experience the process, but it has incredible power here inside the company," he said. It was, in short, a statement of shared purpose, created by all constituencies in the community. And, furthermore, it was a description of a higher purpose, not to shift engines from shelf to shelf but to make people's lives better and, at the same time, put to productive work the incredible power and creativity of the Cummins workforce of twenty-eight thousand people.

The values process also spurred a change in company name. "One of the things that came out of the exercise," Solso told us, "was that Columbus and the engine business, where the engine business is headquartered, were first among equals." So the decision was made to change the name from Cummins Engine Company, Inc., to Cummins, Inc. The effect, Solso remembered, was "enormous. I would have never anticipated. It was a shot heard around the world."

Outsiders may find it difficult to understand just what a dramatic effect the name change had, but Solso explained that the single word *engine* had taken on incredible significance over the years. It seemed to state that the company's primary mission was engine creation and excluded all other activities as sidelines. He told us that the focus groups asked, "If we're not part of the engine business, do we have any rights?" There could be no sense of shared purpose when many in the company spent their days engaged in work that was not making engines. The changed name opened up new possibilities for people around the world and told them that they were part of a global community.

The vision and values work began the transformation of Cummins's strategic identity from a parochial maker of truck engines into a global provider of power-related goods and services. To accelerate this change, Solso launched a process for more explicitly redefining Cummins's strategy and getting people aligned around it. This too was a highly collaborative effort, starting first with the senior management team and the members of the board of directors. They defined five broad planks of the corporate strategy, which the individual businesses could then interpret to develop and detail their own strategies.

The process created a direct connection from "guiding principles, corporate strategy, business strategy, business objectives" all the way to individual goals, Solso explained. The result is that every manager in the company, no matter where in the world or in what unit he or she operates, should have a work plan that includes activities and objectives that relate back to the corporate plan, and understand his or her role in contributing to the overall collective purpose. "That took about four years to get in place," Solso remembered, "but it created alignment."

In retrospect, Solso was wise to have engaged employees so widely in the development of vision, mission, values, and strategy. The resulting involvement and commitment strengthened the social fabric and enabled Cummins to weather some very tough actions that might otherwise have torn the company apart. In response to the dramatic downturn in the heavy truck market Solso and Cummins leadership laid off some 25 percent of the workforce, began a cost-cutting program and a Six Sigma quality improvement initiative, and restructured the truck business. Most significant, Solso closed the original diesel engine manufacturing plant in Columbus. The closure was so shocking to the Cummins community that Solso said he "needed a bodyguard for six months." But Solso got through the period of turmoil, as did Cummins, because employees recognized that such actions were necessary if the company was to succeed in its new purpose of offering solutions that improved people's lives.

The simultaneous solve—the reforging of community through the shared process of defining values, redefining identity, and aligning goals, combined with the tough business moves—delivered remarkable results. "In the second half of 2003," Solso said, "the ice broke, and we started to see financial results. And then 2004, '05, and '06, each has been a record year." The financial results are quite startling. The company's net sales dropped from about $6.6 billion in 1999 to $5.8 billion in 2002 and then began to climb: $6.2 billion in 2003, $8.4 billion in 2004, $9.9 billion in 2005, to $14.3 billion in 2008. From a $100 million loss in 2000, net income rose sharply along with rising sales, to some $750 million in 2008. In 2007, Solso told us, "We made over $1 billion of EBIT. If you'd asked me three years earlier, if I would think we'd ever make $1 billion EBIT, I would never have believed it." In addition, after the plant closings and dropping from twenty-eight thousand employees in 2000 to twenty-four thousand in 2002, overall employment at Cummins increased significantly to thirty-five thousand in 2009.

Catalyzed by Solso's leadership, Cummins has transformed itself from a Columbus-centric builder of diesel engines into a global community of shared purpose, and one that has substantially outperformed both the S&P 500 and an index of peer companies for the five years from 2005 through the end of 2009.

We believe that the ability of leaders such as Solso to create vibrant global communities is fundamental to the success they achieve. In renewing and strengthening these communities, higher-ambition leaders:

- Unleash the energy of their people and increase commitment to the overall success of their firms by:
    - Giving voice to personal aspirations and values
    - Establishing a meaningful higher purpose

- Reduce organizational friction and enhance collaboration by:
    - Strengthening connections across boundaries
    - Making diversity a source of advantage

Give Voice to Personal Aspirations and Values: "Unleashing the Power"

Solso's success in "unleashing the power of Cummins" demonstrates the extraordinary level of commitment that a leader can create when allowing individuals to voice their personal aspirations and values and see these reflected in the enterprise to which they have devoted their professional lives. This kind of collective process shifts the basis of commitment from allegiance to an individual leader (Solso), a product (diesel engines), or a place (Columbus, Indiana) to a more enduring sense of shared purpose and direction.

As the first CEO of Bright Horizons, after a pair of charismatic founders, David Lissy had to confront directly the question of how to build an enduring commitment to the company as a whole rather than just to its leaders. The husband-and-wife team of Linda Mason and Roger Brown had founded Bright Horizons in 1986 to address employers' need to ensure access to high-quality child care for their employees. By 2001, when Lissy took over, the company had grown to operate over three hundred child-care centers with over nine thousand employees.

"A lot of the cultural strengths were really on the backs of the founders," Lissy recalled, sustained by their personal characters and relationships. "My role, in strong partnership with our president and COO, was to create more systematic ways to really build culture and to sustain culture, not from the bully pulpit of the founder, but more grassroots from the ground up." This was essential, not just because the founders were stepping back from day-to-day involvement, but because the scope of the business was rapidly exceeding the reach of any individual.

"Our service is such an intensely human service," Lissy observed, that both the people and the culture are critical to success. The company was therefore built "on the self-fulfilling prophecy that if you take care of your employees, treat them well, and you develop a culture, ultimately that allows you to perform well in the market," he added.

"What we have done differently than when it was founder-led," Lissy told us, "was to really create a much, much wider network of people who are gatekeepers of the mission, people who are the evangelists of the company and mission, keepers of the flame, and to do that at really all levels of the company." Lissy and the leadership team have created those "keepers of the flame" through a combination of giving them a voice in shaping the community, supporting them in seeing the community as a place where they can achieve their full potential, and creating accountability.

Lissy stressed the importance of values, referring to them as verbs—the actions we expect of one another:

> A powerful turning point for us was when we said, "You know what, we have no real substantive way to codify, not the noun or the objective of the company, but the verbs, the actions that we expect of one another." Because that's what people are really looking for when we're trying to introduce them to the Bright Horizons culture. They can buy the rhetoric of the mission and look at all that as what we all aspire towards, but really what they want to know is "How do we work together? What are the ground rules?"

So we developed the Heart Principles. We put together a task force of people at every level of the company to do this exercise— teachers, directors, people in the home office, regional managers, all levels. And we just essentially said, tell us what those things are.

Out of that work emerged a one-page statement of fifteen principles, a guide to "help us support one another and reflect the spirit of our company in the important work we do each day."[1] Its power was in distilling and expressing community norms. "For the most part, everything that's in the Heart Principles already existed," Lissy told us. "It was just a way to get common language and common unity."

Lissy explained that the Heart Principles have been widely embraced, because they provide leaders throughout the organization with a "common language." Lissy recounted his experience from a recent trip: "I was in Aberdeen, Scotland. I go into a faculty lounge and I see the Heart Principles up on the wall. Everybody has picked out their favorite principle and written a situation that's happened at work that correlates to one of the principles."

Lissy explained how he himself uses the principles as part of the orientation for new child-care center directors. After a morning learning about Bright Horizons' history, "they come to my house, and I cook them lunch and I talk to them. And I always ask them, 'Tell me which Heart Principle resonates with you most as a leader and why?' It's a great way to have a conversation."

"The best thing about this," in Lissy's view, "has been how the Heart Principles have become part of our speech. People will say, 'That's inconsistent with the Heart Principles.'"

Steven Holtzman, founding CEO of Infinity Pharmaceuticals, a biotech start-up, talked with us about the power of providing voice in shaping the values of the enterprise for a quite different population than that at Bright Horizons—PhD scientists. He described the challenges in biotech as "scientists coming out of the academy, where there's a culture which is all about the individual—my idea, my experiment, my paper." He sought to build something different, something "that's a lot like a really tight jazz group: they're individual improvisers, and yet, at the same time, the music that they're making is only possible and inspired by the group."

To address this challenge, he connected the concept of "voice" to a deeper notion of "citizenship." The challenge he put to the Infinity staff: "How do we make this the place where you can do your best work?" He told us, "Basically, I keep saying to the people, 'That's a function of you. It's your community. What it's like here—I have an influence, but you have as much, a different kind of influence.' So, putting the responsibility back into their hands to create a kind of community in which they want to stay."

The key in Holtzman's view is to "create an organization in which there are clear roles and there's clear leadership, and yet at the same time, everyone has a fundamental sense of autonomy, in terms of realizing their own potential and contributing as part of a community whose primary value is dedicated to making new medicines." The result, in Holtzman's words: "It's a community and a business. It's both."

Paul Bulcke, CEO of Nestlé, spoke about his organization of 280,000 people in terms that were remarkably similar to Holtzman's description of a biotech start-up. Bulcke summed up Nestlé's attraction this way: "First, people can realize themselves"—that is, develop to their potential in whatever area. "Second, and even more important, they can be themselves in values." They read the management and leadership principles and say, according to Bulcke, "Well, that's me. I don't have to read it and to remember it and not to forget to act like A, B, C. No, I can just be myself." It is a special thing, he observed, "in the world of today, to be in a company that grows, and you feel proud to be part of it, but you can be yourself, and stay true to your own principles and values."

Bulcke, like other higher-ambition CEOs, noted that a hard edge of accountability for acting according to values is critical. This is one area where these leaders are absolutely uncompromising. To receive a promotion at Nestlé, Bulcke told us, it is very important "how you walk the talk towards these leadership principles." And if someone is not leading in a way that is consistent with the values, Bulcke said, "We have to act. But you never act against the person. It's very dangerous to do something *against* something. You do it *for* something. You do it for the organization, for the 279,999 others."

Establish a Meaningful Higher Purpose: "Here for Good"

Perhaps the most fundamental element that binds a higher-ambition enterprise together into a community, rather than simply an economic entity, is its commitment to a purpose beyond the immediate financial goals of the business. This commitment includes but goes well beyond corporate social responsibility. This purpose—it might even be thought of as a corporate calling—means serving a public interest in the core of what higher-ambition enterprises do as a firm. We saw that purpose in Nokia's belief in the potential, especially in developing countries, to change people's lives by how they communicate and in Becton Dickinson's vision to be as well known as the Red Cross for its contributions to global health.

Making a larger contribution helps build trust in a firm's brands and reputation and often makes it easier for higher-ambition firms such as SCB, Cummins, Nokia, Volvo, and Italcementi to do business in a range of countries and cultures. For example, Carlo Pesenti, the heir and CEO of the Italian cement manufacturer Italcementi, commented, "What we are now reading in books about sustainability has been in our company for many years. The cement industry has environmental impact and affects the local neighborhoods in terms of resources and logistics. We need to live in these markets, to start to share views with the people living in these markets, and to build up positive long-term relationships with the local communities to get our license to operate. It's critical." These firms, in other words, are building social capital not just with their employees, but also with their customers and with the communities in which they operate by doing good.

However, it is clear from the consistency and intensity with which higher-ambition leaders covered this topic in our interviews that their commitment to creating and pursuing a higher sense of purpose for the enterprise was about something far more fundamental for them than just improving brand image. This sense of larger purpose provides a positive basis for identifying with the firm—for defining "this is who we are," and "this is what we stand for." It helps employees realize that they are capable of great things, which energizes them to perform better and take on more in their work and lives beyond the workplace. For example, Solso explained that there is a core belief and value at Cummins that "you are only as healthy as the communities in which you live and work. If they're not healthy, you're not healthy. So it is in our self-interest to be active in the community. That is one of the top reasons why people come to the company and why they want to be here. They can do more than just make money."

Let us return to SCB to explore the interplay among social value, economic value, and the reinforcement of the bank's internal culture and community. In the spring of 2010, SCB came out with a bold statement of its brand promise: "Here for good." CEO Peter Sands told us, "The nice thing about the phrase is that it captures two things that we think are very important. One is the durability, the sense of commitment, as epitomized in the way that we thought about our existing clients during the crisis. It's a philosophy about banking based on long-term relationships."

The second meaning? Sands explained, "It is, of course, a normative one. We actually are very serious about our social purpose." Sands told us, as a leading bank in major emerging economies, "we think we play a very important role in the economy, and we want to make sure that we make a positive impact on society and the broader economy." Sands spoke directly about how this concern for creating social value fits with delivering economic returns. It stands, "not in opposition or alongside what we do to create shareholder value, but is integrally connected with what we're doing," he said.

Making such a bold public commitment was a direct response to the posteconomic crisis. "At a time when everything about the durability of banks—their permanence, their values—was being questioned," Sands told us, "we wanted to go on the 'front foot' with our commitment to being here for good and our commitment to doing the right thing. We wanted to be out there, holding ourselves to a standard of playing a positive role in society, and saying, 'We are going to test our business decisions against whether or not they are the right thing to do from a social usefulness, normative point of view.'"

Sands recognized that going public in this way and declaring a standard means that, inevitably, the bank will be judged against it: "We recognize that there's an edge to it. When we do something that's controversial, people will say, 'Well, hang on, you said you were here for good.'" Sands was clear on the challenge: "We won't please everybody all the time, particularly on the normative aspect. Building a mine, for example, creates jobs but also creates some environmental damage." But Sands embraced the challenge: "We need to make very explicit in our own decision making how we're holding ourselves to that standard. We have a reputational risk committee that looks at any transaction with a potentially controversial aspect to it, and we do turn down a lot of transactions, but also we want everyone, every day, to be also making those types of decisions and trade-offs."

Sands noted that this was an internal commitment as much as an external one. "What we're trying to do is ratchet up the cultural bias towards doing the right thing—sticking with our clients, sticking with our commitments," he said. The effort has indeed influenced decision making within the bank. "'Here for good' means that we don't enter a new market lightly, because if we were to leave those markets it would be a very serious thing. Similarly, you don't take on new customers lightly, because implicit in the 'Here for good' promise is that we'll stand by you through good times and bad," said Sands.

Sands and the leadership team looked for a tangible way that all employees could feel they were in an organization that was very serious about its role in the community and in society. "We've always had an employee volunteering program, where people get two days' worth of time they can dedicate to being an employee volunteer. We upped it to three days and made a much more concerted program to provide people with the tools so they could very easily find interesting opportunities to be a volunteer," he said.

The program has been a big success. Sands reeled off the numbers from a report on his desk: there had been 11,800 volunteer days in 2009; this had risen to 49,000 in 2010. He commented, "What we wanted was a quick, powerful way of making everybody feel like they were doing something 'Here for good' and that the organization was serious about it. We don't want people to think 'Here for good' is just about community responsibility; on the other hand, community responsibility is part of it. The core of it is that the way the bank runs should be 'Here for good.'"

Chairman Ratan Tata addressed similar themes when he described the way the Tata Group has brought together its philanthropic and commercial efforts for the purpose of making a better world. A commitment to confronting poverty has been a part of the Tata Group's identity and core values virtually since its founding. So Tata was surprised that, as his company grew globally, such activities came under unaccustomed scrutiny. "We'd never had a question raised about this being something we couldn't afford until we started having foreign shareholders," Tata said. "It sounds like we were very naive, but it did surprise us."

The Tata Group gives 4 percent of its profits to the community. It also supports volunteer groups, like the Disaster Relief Committee, that are formed around an immediate need and disbanded once the need has been met. "For example," Tata said, "when there was a tsunami, every employee of the Tata group, all three hundred thousand of them, gave one day's wages.

Tata Group normally would match that, but doubled the amount because of the calamity. Another committee was formed of volunteers from different Tata companies, and we gave them leave to go and work in these calamity areas. We bought boats. We created an orphanage for children who had lost their parents. We created skills for the women who'd lost their husbands. And then the committee disbanded and everybody went back to work."

Like other leaders in this chapter, Tata's vision for the group's social contribution extends beyond support of social causes to the commercial aspects of the organization. Tata was so engaged by this topic that he continued our conversation well beyond the appointed time for our interview.

A project that particularly excited Tata was the Nano, the company's latest car model. The Nano has attracted attention for its remarkably low price (a bit over $2,000). In the press, Tata has spoken about the idea of a "people's car" that will make transportation affordable to India's lower classes. In particular, as he told us, "What motivated the Nano project was seeing families of four and five people riding a scooter together. I thought that was dangerous." This personal motivation was, of course, coupled with a financial opportunity. Tata told us he believed there was a market for a million Nanos in India each year.

Tata also spoke about an even more ambitious vision for the Nano: to establish young entrepreneurs who would set up plants across India and become Nano assemblers in a given territory. There would be two benefits of this plan, as Tata explained: "First, we would reach a segment of the market that hadn't been reached and hopefully improve the quality of life for those people. Second, we would create a new band of entrepreneurs who would employ a group of people, give them skills, and create a new business ecosystem."

Many higher-ambition CEOs have found that mobilizing the organization around a meaningful purpose can reinforce the group's sense of community. It also offers an advantage as an employer in hiring the best people. Brian Walker of Herman Miller sees that incoming employees "want a deeper meaning in their life. They're not going to be willing just to show up and do what you tell them to do. So to me, it seems fairly simple that one of the things we have to do is we have to figure out how to get to a greater level of purpose."

Strengthen Connections Across Boundaries: Beyond Hub and Spoke

In addition to building commitment through shared values and a meaning-ful purpose, higher-ambition CEOs heavily emphasized strengthening col-laboration across boundaries. Many of these leaders' firms are responding to the new demands of becoming truly global in their approach. For some, like French building materials manufacturer Lafarge, this has meant ex-panding from a base with the majority of revenues in France to becoming a truly global player with 80 percent of revenues coming from over seventy other countries in the space of fifteen years. For a number of others, such as SCB, IKEA, and Cummins, with an extensive geographic footprint already established, it meant changing their approach to competing internationally.

Even for Nestlé, the epitome of a longtime international player, with less than 2 percent of its sales in its home market of Switzerland, there is a changing global dynamic. "The developing world is developing—at last," Bulcke told us. "Developing on their own terms. They're not just trying to copy Western countries any more. That's over. Western countries don't fully understand that yet."

Many of these companies are seeking ways to leverage global scale and also to achieve local focus, and are adopting hybrid organizing models with strong global products or functions, combined with strong geographic accountability. Recall, for example, SCB's strong/strong organizing ap-proach that gave significant power to both the lines of business and the country CEOs.

Higher-ambition leaders understand that the informal connections and social relationships at the heart of community are key to getting these new organizational forms to work. SCB, for example, goes to great lengths to move people around geographically and across functional areas, asking people to step up to new challenges outside their previous experience. According to Sands, the bank has taken risks to build a rich web of relationships and mutual understanding across the organization. For example, as we mentioned in chapter 2, SCB placed a non-lawyer as head of the legal and compliance function and promoted the leader of the organizational learning group to CEO of the China business.

Higher-ambition companies frequently use project teams as a fast, targeted way to build personal networks. IKEA, for example, staffs project teams with employees from the different local units rather than building up resources at headquarters. When the project is complete, the people return to their unit with new knowledge and broadened relationships across the enterprise. Similarly, Italcementi uses multinational task forces to develop and integrate operations. It does this to ensure that it is developing its systems and technologies to the same standards and with the same level of attention to environmental issues, irrespective of location.

SCB's approach to acquisition integration is a particularly striking example of investing in building personal networks. As we described earlier, when the bank acquired additional operations in Taiwan, it selected sixty ambassadors from the new Taiwanese entity to make 'getting to know you' visits to thirty other countries, conducting events with the local SCB staff and with members of the local business communities. The ambassadors brought back an understanding of the bank's operations in, say, Uganda or Malaysia, as well as relationships that could facilitate doing business together. The goal, said Sands, is to "accelerate the process of bringing them in and making them part of the same seamless whole."

SCB seeks other ways to reinforce the bank's natural networks so they can connect individuals and groups. We talked earlier about the use of thematic phone calls to target specific communities, such as one on International Women's Day and another to mark the fiftieth anniversary of

Ghana's independence. SCB also expects that people will contribute beyond their own area of work. Sands explained, "Everyone knows that they should be doing things that extend beyond their role within their particular function or country, and that they should show some leadership to the bank as a whole." For example, a manager in India might share an understanding of some particularly successful initiative or idea so that someone else could use it in her function or geographic area.

Sands also pointed out the importance of encouraging people to reach out and bring in good ideas: "We recognize people not just for coming up with good ideas, but for being smart in picking them up and running with them. Rewarding the picking up is important." Each time that an idea is shared effectively, it reinforces the cultural glue and weakens the not-invented-here syndrome that plagues most organizations.

These efforts to build social relationships throughout the network strengthen global integration in a distinctive way. At SCB, Cummins, Nestlé, and others, higher-ambition CEOs spoke of moving away from a hub-and-spoke model of international operations in which the dominant channels for moving information and people are between the center and the individual units. Instead, they distribute resources and leadership capacity directly across the network, from point to point, without having to pass through headquarters in, say, Columbus, Indiana, or Vevey, Switzerland. Leif Johansson observed that, as Volvo's customers become increasingly global, the company must be able to harness its worldwide capabilities to respond to customer demands, wherever the customer might be.

Make Diversity a Source of Advantage: "Respect Is Incredibly Important"

Embracing diversity is a distinctive feature of the new form of community that higher-ambition leaders are working to create. Indeed, one of the most striking findings in all our conversations with these leaders was their passion for the topic of diversity. This passion was rooted both in values and in a pragmatic understanding of the capabilities required to win in an increasingly complex, global context.

Johansson went so far as to say that "diversity is what we are about. We are trying to make that an attractive part of what Volvo is. We are inviting people into the group by saying that if you're interested in diversity, if you thrive on diversity, if you like different foods, if you like to travel, and if you like to speak the global language of bad English, come to us, because that's what we are about." (More on the significance of bad English later.)

Volvo has not always seen diversity as a source of strength. When Johansson took over as CEO in 1997, he faced a situation much like the one Solso found at Cummins. He realized that Volvo's dominant Swedish culture—its Mecca was Gothenburg—was so strong and so self-certain as to make all others within the global organization subservient. This tendency showed up most powerfully when it came to mergers and acquisitions. "We believed we were so unique and special that, when we acquired a company, what we did was actually destroy it," Johansson said, "because we were sure that they couldn't have been doing anything right."

When we spoke to Johansson in 2007, he told us that "respect for the individual" is what made it possible for Volvo to change its ways. In his opinion, it is the only way to handle acquisitions. "We are all colleagues, whether we happen to be a French colleague, a Swedish colleague, or an American colleague," he said. "It is very important that you don't talk about Frenchmen as Frenchmen, natives of Gothenburg as natives of Gothenburg, or Americans as Americans. You need to talk about them as brilliant development engineers."

It's also essential that all colleagues speak the same language, and, at Volvo, Johansson decreed that the mother tongue would be "bad English." His belief is that people who speak less-than-perfect English often do a better job of building connections with their colleagues from other cultures than native English speakers who pay close attention to the grammatical niceties. "Bad English works much better than advanced English," he told us in a round table discussion among CEOs held in Gothenburg. "Perfect English has too many words for people in a global company to understand."

Solso was equally passionate about diversity. For him, embracing diversity could be a source of advantage in attracting and retaining talent. Probably the most important thing, he told us, that will allow Cummins to take its game to the next level is "creating the right environment. By that I mean that we are seen as a place people want to come to work. It looks like the United Nations. It's inclusive and welcoming and people have the opportunity to develop their full potential."

Lissy echoed the same theme: "Diversity has always been a strong value of Bright Horizons from the very beginning, but we just sort of let it ride and have it be happenstance. A few years ago, we said, 'Look, we're drawing a line in the sand. We're going to be more deliberate about some of this stuff, because we're not happy that the diversity of the management of the company is not reflective of the diversity of the people who work for us.' We've got a hugely diverse workforce, but we didn't have a very diverse management team."

As we explored why diversity was so important to these leaders, we learned that it was not simply about inclusion, but about a different way of working together. Solso observed, "You need to move people beyond race and gender and into a broader sense of how we want to work together." At the heart of these leaders' work on diversity was creating respect for the individual and cultivating a genuine belief that better answers will come from tapping the wisdom of the group. They wanted their people to be proactive about seeking to understand and benefit from the perspectives of others.

The concern for diversity also reflects an awareness that the dominant culture, whatever it is, can too easily squeeze out divergent perspectives that are valuable—even essential—to success. For Bang & Olufsen, the high-end Danish consumer entertainment products firm, the dominant culture in 2001 was that of the product designers and mechanical engineers. These were the people, working in IdeaLand—B&O's concept development center—who came up with the sleek designs for its high-end speakers and audio electronics products.

The CEO who took over at that time, Torben Ballegaard Sørensen, told us of his challenges in bringing in the new software-focused developers who were critical to the next generation of products. "We put the software designers right smack in the middle of IdeaLand," he said, "but we found that some of their creativity dried up. That's because the software-oriented people, who generate virtual ideas, did not enjoy a great deal of prestige in the mechanistic, heavy-aluminum environment. When the physical people feel that they are the bosses, bringing something virtual into a physical environment and getting it to catch on is not a simple matter."

Ballegaard Sørensen felt the only way to protect the software people was to provide them with some separation: "We felt we had to place that organism in another environment that had a life of its own, until it was strong enough to stand up to the dominant, aluminum gene. So, it was really an organizational tool to make this little weed flower grow and be strong enough to keep up with the old, strong sunflower it was standing next to."

By 2007, Ballegaard Sørensen concluded he could "put them back together in the same room, so that people will use the same loos, and eat in the same canteens. We can do so now, because the new embryo is strong enough to resist the antibodies from the old being."

The CEOs we spoke with embrace diversity because they are convinced that it is a route to superior collaboration, both within their organizations and across external boundaries, whether with joint ventures or recent acquisitions.

Solso noted that superior collaboration is at the very heart of the company's strategy. "Nine of our top-ten customers make their own engines. So the question is, why do we exist?" Why would Cummins's customers choose to purchase a product from Cummins rather than make it themselves in one of their other divisions? Partly, he explained, it's because Cummins provides technology advantages along with a global distribution and services footprint. But in large measure, he told us, it is because Cummins has a superior capability to establish a "partnership relationship with customers, rather than the typical vendor relationship." Similarly, Cummins is better at joint ventures. "This is very different," he told us, contrasting Cummins's approach with that of competitors. "We don't have to control the thing. Whether it's 51-49 or 50-50, it doesn't matter." What matters is the respect for each party, the ability to collaborate, and the shared commitment to the venture's success.

As one indication of just how serious Solso has been about diversity, a colleague noted that in seven years of chairing Cummins's diversity council, Solso did not miss a single meeting, and only once did he briefly step out of a meeting to take an urgent call.

Conclusion

In many ways, the capacity to develop and sustain the enterprise as a vibrant social community is the "secret sauce" that powers the success of higher-ambition leaders and their companies. By giving people voice in a way that builds their personal identification with the community, building deep respect for individual diversity, finding multiple ways to connect across organizational boundaries, and creating a shared purpose around building a better world, they develop high levels of commitment and increase the capacity to collaborate (see table 5-1).

In turn, this allows leaders to distribute responsibility far into the company and to organize in a way that requires people to collaborate across boundaries, and trusts and demands them to do so. Higher-ambition CEOs reduce the tensions and organizational friction that often occur in a complex matrix by building a tight fabric of social relationships, shortening the psychological distance between different parts of the organization, and creating collective commitment to the firm's strategy and purpose. They also increase strategic adaptability and innovation by building the capacity to productively manage diversity and increasing the lateral flows of ideas and perspectives. What differentiates these companies from less successful global companies, which also have matrix structures, is the global community that these leaders have created.

TABLE 5-1

Creating community out of diversity

	HIGHER-AMBITION LEADERS' APPROACH	
Common leadership pattern	Management "best practices"	Additional distinctive practices
GIVE VOICE TO PERSONAL ASPIRATIONS AND VALUES		
• Corporate values are developed and posted	• Statement of vision and values is widely understood • People who do not fit values are replaced	• There is a strong connection between personal and corporate values • The whole organization is involved in developing and refreshing values • Values are central to decisions about hiring and promotions
ESTABLISH A MEANINGFUL HIGHER PURPOSE		
• Corporate objectives are framed primarily in financial terms	• The company sets high standards for integrity and ethical conduct • There is a genuine commitment to corporate social responsibility	• Company's approach to its businesses embodies a higher purpose • Higher purpose is an important part of "the glue" that brings diverse people together into a shared community
STRENGTHEN CONNECTIONS ACROSS BOUNDARIES		
• Primary allegiance is to a single function or unit • Silos and stovepipes are common	• Individuals are expected to act in line with the greater interest of the company and community • Active efforts are made to work across silos (e.g., by serving on teams and taking temporary assignments) • Forums bring together extended leadership team to improve alignment and develop informal personal relationships	• Individuals are expected to proactively reach out and contribute ideas and resources across the organization • Multiple reinforcing mechanisms, both formal and informal, are used to deepen personal connections and social relationships

	HIGHER-AMBITION LEADERS' APPROACH	
Common leadership pattern	**Management "best practices"**	**Additional distinctive practices**
MAKING DIVERSITY A SOURCE OF ADVANTAGE		
• Efforts to increase employee diversity are driven by the human resources function and are strongly linked to legal requirements	• Minority employees are recruited and encouraged	• Understanding of and respect for different cultural perspectives and personal viewpoints are proactively promoted
		• The company's successful focus on diversity is used as a source of advantage in recruitment, retention, and innovative collaboration
		• Diversity seen as a source for effective response to diverse markets

6

Leading with *Sisu*

I just finally learned, if you pick one or two things, and drive it
for four or five years, good things will happen.

—Tim Solso, Cummins Inc.

I N THE PREVIOUS CHAPTERS, we have described the work of
higher-ambition leaders in crafting a compelling strategic identity,
delivering on the performance expectations of key stakeholders,
and building a global community of shared purpose out of diversity—all of
which present highly demanding leadership challenges. In this chapter, we
will describe the practices that allow higher-ambition CEOs to successfully
meet these leadership challenges.

Consider the challenges that Volvo's Leif Johansson has faced for over
a decade. The stage for Johansson's recruitment to Volvo was set by the
downfall of an illustrious predecessor. On December 3, 1993, Pehr G
Gyllenhammar—"Mr. Volvo," Volvo's chairman, earlier CEO (1971–1990),
and the highest-paid executive in Sweden at the time—was forced to
resign.

Gyllenhammar had been the principal architect of a proposed merger
with Renault, then wholly owned by the French government, but undergoing a process of privatization. Under the proposed deal, Volvo would have

merged its automotive operations with those of Renault to create the world's sixth-largest car and truck maker, with Volvo retaining a 35 percent stake in the combined entity. But arguments grew increasingly heated within Sweden—and, crucially, within Volvo—that one of the country's most important companies was being sold off to foreigners too cheaply and without sufficient regard for the interests of Swedish workers or Swedish industry. The revelation that the French government would keep a "golden share," which meant it could retain control of the proposed merged company for the foreseeable future, provoked even more vociferous objections from the important Swedish newspapers and Volvo's strong unions, as well as from managers within Volvo, who wrote open letters to the company's senior leadership urging them not to pursue the deal.

As the date approached for the shareholder vote of approval, several of Volvo's largest shareholders announced that they would oppose the merger. Then, at a hastily convened meeting, Sören Gyll, Volvo's managing director, announced that many of Volvo's top executives objected to the deal: Gyllenhammar's position was untenable. He resigned, followed by four other board members.

In the wake of the failed merger, Volvo struggled to find direction. In 1997, it recruited Johansson to provide fresh leadership. Less than two years later, in January 1999, to the shock and dismay of most of Sweden, he sold off the car division to Ford Motor Company, as we discussed earlier. There was even more dismay when, in 2001, he led the acquisition of Renault Trucks for $1.7 billion in shares. With fresh memories of the disastrous merger attempt just eight years before, most commentators predicted the same painful clash of cultures and interests.

The two deals sent shock waves through Swedish industry and the broader society. Johansson was called a traitor—and worse. Johansson and his team, however, knew that the industrial logic was crystal clear. The automotive, truck, and heavy equipment industries would continue to consolidate and globalize, driven by the potential for scale economies in engines and in the supply chain. Volvo simply didn't have the resources or the capital required to achieve these scale economies in both automobiles and trucks. Volvo could either figure out a way to become a leading global player or resign itself to increasing marginalization. Johansson and his team chose the former and embarked on a decade-long struggle of integration efforts to create a company capable of competing at a world-class level.

Why was Johansson able to succeed where Gyllenhammar had failed? What established Johansson's personal legitimacy and influence so that he could make such wrenching decisions, both to sell the car division and to integrate subsequent acquisitions, and still carry the organization with him? What was required of him personally to lead through the dislocation and disruption of consolidating two proud national champions, Volvo and Renault, into a leading global player?

As we shall describe, Johansson's experience at Volvo illustrates the broader findings from our research on higher-ambition leaders. Behind the unique aspects of personal character and specific company context, we found a distinctive quality, which we believe is best captured by the Finnish word, *sisu*. *Sisu* refers to the courage, will, perseverance, and endurance that allow a person to do such things as walk for hours in meter-deep snow with the hope and conviction that there is a warm house at the end of the journey. *Sisu* also refers to becoming strong together—as a collective—and to something internal, an inner strength that helps you to keep focused through danger and hard times and that helps you to relentlessly pursue a distant goal. In Finland, *sisu* is more than a characteristic, it is a virtue. Nokia's Jorma Ollila, a Finn, refers to *sisu* as "guts."

When we take a step back from our research and look at the stories we have collected from CEOs around the world, we see these leaders are taking their organizations on multiyear journeys through demanding territory. To enable their organizations to successfully navigate the difficult, often unforeseen challenges along the way, these leaders need to demonstrate the grit, persistence, and focus that are the essence of *sisu*.

Volvo: From National Icon to Global Competitor

The Volvo board of directors selected Johansson in 1997 as a chief executive in large part because it believed he had the vision and perseverance to achieve the company's long-term goals. "I was hired," Johansson told Flemming Norrgren and Tobias Fredberg, "because the board had reached the conclusion that someone who could apply a long-term perspective was required. As the chairman of the board, Bert-Olof Svanholm, explained, 'we want Leif, because Leif is capable of seeing this as his mission in life.'"

Though he came in as an outsider, Johansson was no stranger to Volvo. He has deep roots in Volvo and in Gothenburg, Volvo's home city. His father, Lennart, was a legendary CEO of the roller-bearing company SKF, which founded Volvo in the mid-1920s. Johansson grew up in central Gothenburg and graduated from the city's engineering school, Chalmers University. He had a very successful career at Electrolux, a globalizing manufacturer of home appliances and white goods, where he rose to become president in 1991 and CEO in 1994. All this experience made him an obvious candidate for the job.

Johansson met with us in Volvo's futuristic head office, which Gyllenhammar had built when he was at the pinnacle of his power. ("I am glad I have it, but also glad I didn't build it," said Johansson.) Gazing out from the elegant structure that stands on a hilltop overlooking Volvo's production facilities, Johansson gestured. "Everyone from Gothenburg always assumes that you want to come back," he said. "Poor guy, he has been in Stockholm all this time, we should bring him home!"

Johansson came into the job knowing that he faced several important challenges. First, he needed to reestablish a stronger operational role for the CEO and group management. In anticipation of the planned 1993 merger with Renault, Volvo had created divisions and severed the ties between cars, trucks, buses, and construction equipment to enable each unit to merge with the corresponding unit in Renault. Despite the failure of the merger, Volvo kept the structure and increasingly adopted the character of a holding company. "Expressed in a somewhat dramatic way," Johansson explained, "I think you could say that the Volvo head office had abdicated." Johansson knew there would be a need to share resources across the divisions and to drive a lower-cost operating model.

He was also clear that he would take power back from the division heads, who had become accustomed to participating in meetings between management and the board. But, recalled Johansson, "When I joined Volvo, the board—and I myself—stated clearly that now we have a CEO, and he must bear the responsibility of deciding how things should be done. If we need information about trucks, we'll invite the head of trucks to join us, but the head of trucks will not be attending the whole meeting." It was no longer going to be a "representative democracy," but a "proper unification of the group."

Johansson also expected to make acquisitions and knew he needed to create a Volvo culture that could successfully integrate other companies. And he knew that he had to resolve fundamental questions about the future of the car division, which had been bleeding money for the better part of two decades.

Early on, Johansson took three actions intended to establish his leadership and reset Volvo's direction.

The first was a simple, symbolic act that quickly signaled a results-focused willingness to challenge the status quo: tax consolidation. Until then, Volvo's legal structure had followed its divisional operating structure, with the resulting fiscal disadvantage that it could not aggregate results and consolidate taxes for each country. By consolidating, the company saved close to $50 million per year in taxes. Johansson also sent a clear signal: "That symbolic act had a very strong effect in that management now understood that the head office intended to grip the reins firmly."

Second, he breathed new life and energy into a values initiative led by a task force of younger employees that had been languishing for some time. Volvo already had a deeply embedded set of core values about quality, safety, and the environment, and the task force had been charged with defining additional future values for how the group should function in psychological and emotional terms. Johansson embraced the work of the task force, which had articulated new values such as energy and passion. He also inserted a value that was meaningful to him—respect for the individual— and that he could see would be critical for the company in the future, particularly in developing its capacity to integrate acquisitions effectively.

Johansson was taking on what he saw as a critical weakness in the Volvo culture, an arrogance and complacency about its own professionalism, which, combined with Swedish chauvinism, gave it a very poor track record as an acquirer. "It was precisely this aspect that we began tackling," Johansson said, "when we identified 'the Volvo way.'"

In January 1998, Johansson launched his third initiative, a strategy process that resulted ultimately in the sale of the car division. He started the process with a personal letter to each of the operating unit heads, laying out the strategic questions that he believed they needed to address. The process made evident the capital requirements for each of the units as well as the fundamental challenge the group faced. Against profits of just over $1 billion, the capital requirements from the units exceeded $7 billion. "We realized," Johansson explained, "that if we were to manage passenger cars and commit so many resources to passenger cars, we wouldn't be able to manage the rest. So we were facing a choice between the rest of the group or continuing with passenger cars." Given the disparity in both performance and outlook between cars and the other businesses, the choice was clear. By January 1999, the sale of the Volvo car division to Ford was complete.

Forging a Global Competitor

Flush with cash from the sale of the car division, Johansson was ready to move rapidly to bulk up the remaining businesses. In the summer of 1999, about six months after the sale of the car division, Volvo made a deal with the powerful Wallenberg family to buy Scania, the other major Swedish truck manufacturer. But on March 14 the following year, the European Union Commission blocked the deal on anticompetitive grounds. Twelve days later, the deal was completely dead: the Wallenberg family sold 34 percent of Scania's shares to Volkswagen.

Johansson saw it was necessary to act fast. Less than a month later, Volvo and Renault reached an agreement on a deal in which Volvo bought Renault Vehicules Industriels (RVI)—Renault's truck division—for $1.7 billion in shares. RVI had ten years earlier bought the U.S.-based Mack Trucks. Together, the Renault and Mack deal changed the nature of Volvo from a Swedish organization with an international presence to a company with global aspirations.

Johansson chose to use the acquisition as the catalyst for a dramatic restructuring. His logic was to gain the benefits of scale in the parts of the business where Volvo could achieve major cost savings, in particular, in the supply chain and in powertrain, where engines can be shared across different kinds of trucks and construction equipment and the same engine can be sold around the globe. If Johansson could pull off the restructuring, it would give Volvo significant competitive advantages. Yet Volvo had to do so while keeping sales and marketing responsive to local customer needs.

"We broke up both Volvo trucks and Renault trucks," he explained, "in terms of the organization structure. We set up a single powertrain division with one single management. Then we set up the 3P organization, which stands for purchasing, product planning, and product development."

"It was a violent change," he continued. Renault trucks, Volvo trucks, and Mack trucks had each formerly been complete units that fully integrated all the functions; after the reorganization, they became responsible just for assembly and sales. The magnitude of the change was too great for the old heads of the truck divisions. "They felt we deprived them of their operational mandate," Johansson told us, "and that was quite true." They all ended up leaving. In Johansson's words, "they didn't want to stay on, as they thought there was too much blood flowing."

But the structural changes unblocked a major competitive advance. By creating a unified powertrain organization, Volvo was able to achieve a dramatic rationalization of its engine platforms, reducing the number from eighteen engine families to just two in a period of five years. In turn, the resulting competitive advantages, as well as those from the globally integrated 3P organization, helped justify continued investments in further acquisitions and alliances, particularly in Asia, including the 2006 acquisition of Japanese truck manufacturer, Nissan Diesel. By then, Johansson felt Volvo had made great strides in becoming a superior acquirer: "We've created a culture that is embracing and inviting to external people who join our company. I think we've managed to establish a culture that permits us to make acquisitions and make progress, if we have the courage."

More than ten years down the road, Volvo has been able to both focus and expand. Almost all the company is based on heavy diesel engines. The sale of the car division in 1999 reduced the group's turnover by 41 percent and the number of employees by 31 percent. But the expansion since then has been dramatic. By 2008, prior to the global economic crisis, turnover had increased by over 140 percent, while the number of employees had increased by 82 percent. From number six in the worldwide truck industry in 1999, Volvo has grown to become the world's second-largest manufacturer of trucks. Similarly, from number eight in construction equipment, Volvo has grown to become the third-largest global player. The combination of global integration via the joint business units (including 3P and powertrain) and adaptation to local markets via the product-related companies has continued. The business units now employ around 30 percent of the group's employees.

Principles of *Sisu* Leadership

While Johansson confronted many widely varying challenges during his tenure at Volvo, from his original need to assert himself in claiming a more operational role for the group, through the sale of the car division, to the heavy work of integrating a series of acquisitions and creating a consolidated global structure, there is an underlying consistency to his leadership approach. The core principles that guide his leadership are remarkably similar to those that characterize the approaches of other higher-ambition leaders:

- *Presence:* Engage and earn trust.

- *Fairness:* Establish a just process.

- *Clarity:* Keep it simple.

- *Persistence:* Stay the course.

Presence: Engage and Earn Trust

Johansson, like many other higher-ambition leaders, asked his people to follow him on a difficult journey. He came in as an outsider and would make a number of difficult changes, starting early in his tenure: changing the operating model to take power back to the center, reshaping the culture to improve Volvo's ability to make acquisitions, and resolving the future of the car division.

In order to earn the required trust, leaders like Johansson invest a great deal of personal effort in direct engagement, putting themselves out there in an emotional sense as well as in direct personal connections. This is particularly important during the phase when they are just taking over or during periods of especially rapid change. But they maintain high levels of personal engagement throughout their tenure.

One of the most powerful ways that higher-ambition leaders earn trust is through direct physical engagement with their people. There is no substitute for the opportunity to take the measure of leaders face to face, to look them in the eye, and judge whether they have earned the right to lead. As we saw earlier, the turning point in an angry mob of employees' acceptance of Anand Mahindra's leadership was his willingness to come out of the back room and directly engage with them, even at the risk of his personal safety.

While Johansson's challenge was a bit less dramatic, he shared a similar view on the importance of physical presence. Johansson told us, "I believe you have to sit as close to it as you bloody well can, right smack in the middle of where things are done, and if you are not prepared to do that, then you shouldn't really be a manager." When Volvo asked Johansson to join in 1997, there was talk of moving headquarters from Gothenburg, on Sweden's west coast where the manufacturing facilities were located, to a larger city. "When I agreed to join, I made it a fundamental condition for doing so that all talk about moving the corporate headquarters to London or Stockholm must cease," he said. In his earlier job with Electrolux, Johansson had learned the importance of being a physical and emotional part of the community of the company. He moved to Gränna, a small Swedish town, located on a beautiful lake between Stockholm and Gothenburg. "You become part of the community and live the same way as everybody else does there," Johansson said. "If you are to be a general, it's quite a good idea to be out there together with the troops."

Johansson also stressed the importance of regularly getting out of the office. He observed, "A culture with a sense of belonging is not created by sitting behind your desk at company headquarters; it is created by you being out there." At the time of the Renault acquisition, for example, he recalled that he had spent a hundred fifty days per year on the road, visiting different parts of the newly combined company.

Direct engagement allows two-way communications, enables continued learning on the part of the CEO, and builds confidence that leadership "gets it"—that the leader genuinely understands the reality that people deep in the organization experience. For engagement to be productive, however, the leader must have an appropriate mind-set, Johansson said. A leader needs to "kick the ball where you find it"—not where you wish it would be. For example, as a newcomer, whether first taking over or making an acquisition, he said, "You don't start by criticizing your predecessor or telling them about all the terrible mistakes they've made. What's done is done, and now we have to move ahead. Embrace the organization and say, 'Now please join in.'"

Engagement is not just about physical presence, but also about establishing an emotional connection. The leader is able to connect his or her personal values with those of the people in the company. Johansson referred to this as one his personal principles: "I don't like dealing with the kinds of things that I personally can't embrace. I have the simple faith that what makes sense for me, makes sense for most people."

For Johansson, the values initiative that was underway when he took office was a way of making this connection. Embracing the values work involved some courage and willingness to take a risk. He highlighted how, in an engineering and financially oriented company, the idea of passion, one of the new values put forward by the task force, generated skepticism at first. "The word *passion* evoked a mixture of jokes and ridicule and evoked very strong feelings in a traditional technical workshop environment," he said. But it connected to his own belief about people needing to find meaning at work. He recalled, with some satisfaction, "As it turned out, this was a success, because this was something that people had actually been longing for. The organization wanted to serve a purpose. This is something which is a feature in me: I want to serve a purpose beyond mere money making."

Engagement is fundamental to building trust and personal legitimacy. People throughout the organization get a chance to judge the leader's character and motivations for themselves. Johansson felt that one of the most important reasons for his success was that people could see from the first that he was totally committed to the company: "They felt that I had no other agenda than to try to make Volvo into a successful company."

The experience of Russ Fradin, who came in as a turnaround CEO at Hewitt Associates (now Aon Hewitt, after Aon's 2010 acquisition of Hewitt Associates), provides a similar illustration of the importance of engagement and earning trust, but in a very different setting from Johansson's heavy industrial business. From its heritage as a highly regarded professional services firm focused on human resources and employment benefits, Hewitt extended in the early 2000s into the racier but riskier business of outsourcing the entire HR function. To raise the capital required to take on large, multiyear outsourcing contracts, Hewitt converted in June 2002 from a private partnership into a publicly traded corporation and then, in 2004, used its shares as currency to buy its leading HR outsourcing competitor, Exult. The results were disastrous. Several of the largest outsourcing contracts were far too aggressively priced, and Hewitt lacked the execution skills to control delivery costs. By the time Fradin was recruited in September 2006, the outsourcing business was reporting losses of $130 million per year.

Fradin was intimately familiar with both consulting and outsourcing. After an eighteen-year consulting career with McKinsey & Company, he had served as a senior executive for seven years at ADP, the global leader in outsourced payroll operations, and two years as CEO at BISYS, a financial services outsourcing company. He even had an insider's view of the HR outsourcing business, having served on the board of Exult, the competitor firm that Hewitt had acquired.

As new leaders typically do, Fradin immediately threw himself into connecting with the organization and with its customers. Early on, he recalled, "I spent probably three-quarters of my time just going around. I think I met with seventy-two clients in the first hundred days, just hearing what they had to say. I went to as many locations as I possibly could domestically and internationally." During his visits, he met with associates in small groups, large groups, one-on-one, "every forum you could imagine, to try to listen. 'What's on your minds?' 'What would you be worried about if you were me?'"

Fradin learned quickly the source of the problems in the outsourcing business: "It became very clear that there just had been a loss of financial discipline." The culture that had made Hewitt so successful in consulting was actually a liability in the outsourcing business. "The old Hewitt mode—we'll do whatever the client asks us to do—really didn't work in the outsourcing world," Fradin said. At successful outsourcers, the account manager must play the bad cop and maintain control of change orders and the scope of work and charge for anything extra; at Hewitt, the account managers were good cops, too willing to accede to client requests, without any corresponding charges.

Fixing the problems, however, would require both painful cost cutting and reshaping some of the fundamental aspects of the firm. Navigating these changes would be particularly challenging, given the professional services setting, where people's motivation and morale are critical not only to performance but to the viability of the institution.

Fradin realized the importance for him to be tightly connected to the organization and to be able to hear, in an unfiltered way, what people were thinking. The classic challenge for a CEO, he observed, is that "a lot of the messages to leadership end up being what people want you to hear." The problem of filtering is in both directions, he explained: "One thing I found when I came in was a very large staff of people in internal communications. For a company of slightly under $3 billion, we had more than thirty people doing internal communications. The messages were being so homogenized and edited so many times, they all kind of looked like Hewitt-speak."

Within three weeks of joining, Fradin decided to create a personal blog. He explained, "Part of the reason I started the blog is I'm perfectly capable of speaking for myself. I don't need thirty-plus people to edit my own words." He concluded that Hewitt didn't need so many of them either, and the department was an early target for cost savings.

Fradin found the blog an important source of organizational insight. Any associate can make a comment on his posts. "It has given me a greater appreciation than I think I've ever had of how the change process affects people's lives," he said. People who had been severed from the company often wrote posts for all the world to see. He continued, "You get a broader view of the organization saying, 'You know, some of this isn't so much fun, Russ. And you should know that.' A lot of times the interesting comment I get is, 'I understand why you're doing what you're doing, and I agree with it, but you should understand it's having the following impact. I'm not happy for this reason, or I'm leaving, or whatever, and you should understand that.'"

Several of the CEOs we spoke to have, like Fradin, used digital media to dramatically increase their ability to engage in direct and unvarnished two-way communication with their people. Ken Freeman, former CEO of Quest Diagnostics and partner at KKR, and now dean of Boston University's business school, spoke about how at Quest he had supplemented the more formal communication systems with a less formal e-mail channel called Ken Direct: "Anybody can share their views. I want to hear from colleagues personally about anything, good, bad, ugly, ideas, concerns, issues, just let me know."

Both Allan Leighton of the Royal Mail and Marjorie Scardino of Pearson have created similar open e-mail channels to encourage employees to make contact. On her first day, Scardino said, she "sent an e-mail saying, 'Hello and here's the kind of company I think I'd like to work for. Is it the kind of company you'd like to work for?'" Ever since, she continued, "I have always sent an e-mail whenever we had results or there's something important, or I think that there's something everybody in the company should know. I think employees should know at exactly the same moment the investors know it."

Scardino described how the two-way communications her e-mails inspired have been a source of ideas and helped make the company seem smaller. Scardino told us: "Sometimes they're really good ideas. So, I try to use them. We have a mechanism for what we do with the ideas and what we do with the people who are angry and that kind of thing. We have different people who are assigned to take care of the different things that come in. A result is that we all kind of feel intimate. There are thirty thousand people here. That's not the biggest company in the world, but it's not small either. But they send me pictures when their children graduate from high school, things like that. It's kind of friendly. That's a great thing."

Leighton told us that he received two hundred e-mails each day via the "Ask Allan" channel, and that this was his key source of understanding what was on the minds of his two hundred thousand employees. His policy was to respond to every e-mail with at least an acknowledgment within fifteen minutes of reception, and follow up with a full answer or reply within seven days. By receiving such a massive amount of e-mails every day, he could more quickly understand and sense key issues that were arising in the organization. Answering quickly is important, he said, "because no one ever believes you actually will answer. Imagine you get two hundred e-mails a day. In a year, you have somehow touched everybody in the organization, because every time you send a note back, they tell twenty people. People think you're the Scarlet Pimpernel. You're everywhere."

Leighton had another form of communication, even more direct. He made unannounced visits to post offices in the United Kingdom when he had the chance. His goal, he said, was to make a link with reality, to listen to employees, and to learn what they needed to be more effective and more engaged in the mission. He told us, "The postmen never said to me, 'You know, we're not investing enough in automation,' or, 'Gosh, our IT plan isn't working.' They said things like, 'When we're out in the rain, our weatherproof jackets leak. And our shoes hurt.' If you're a postman, the most important thing you've got is your bloody feet!"

Engagement involves more than communications; it also depends on how the leader chooses to show up. For Fradin, it was very important to be part of the team: "People work with me and want to be on my team because we will be successful together. I feel much more comfortable in the middle of the parade or at the end of the parade. I usually don't like being at the front of the parade." For Fradin, that meant overcoming the potential barriers created by hierarchical status: "There is an egalitarian streak to me that I think is important. My office is no bigger than anyone else's office, hopefully smaller and dingier. Perks ain't us."

Anu Aga, former executive chair of Thermax, the Indian engineering products firm, believed in the importance of an egalitarian approach for her and her leadership team against the backdrop of Indian corporate culture. "Coming from a country where corporate leaders are very hierarchical and operate from status, we shun ostentation and try our best to be genuine. We remain accessible to employees and encourage an open environment that respects differences," she said.

Engagement and trust enable the CEO to become a focal point for creating shared meaning and shaping the culture. Freeman expressed the point particularly effectively. He reflected on his experience as CEO of Quest Diagnostics, which he took from $350 million in market capitalization when it was spun off from Corning, Inc. at the beginning of 1997, to more than $9 billion when he stepped down in 2004: "I wanted to take a company that was hostile and hierarchical, and not particularly disciplined, and create a values-oriented, honest, disciplined company where the people respected each other. I had to model the behavior at the grassroots level."[1] Trust was central: "If you don't trust your employees and if they don't trust you, cultural change won't happen."

Fairness: Establish a Just Process

Just as higher-ambition leaders invest great energy in engagement and earning trust, they also focus on sustaining trust. Inevitably, as CEOs confront the realities of a dynamic, competitive marketplace, they have to make difficult decisions that will disappoint one or another of their key constituencies and, in some cases, inflict genuine hardship. Aga, who was trained as a social worker, observed, "A leader has to balance the contradiction of being caring, and yet not seek popularity by shunning unpopular, tough decisions."

Johansson spoke of the difficult decisions involved in closing plants and making substantial layoffs, which were an inevitable consequence of Volvo's strategy of globalization and consolidation: "For me, the hardest thing is still to do something that I know will hurt people, although they haven't done anything wrong at all. But this is something I have learned that you have to do. You can't hide from it if you are a company manager."

While they cannot always protect against bad outcomes, higher-ambition leaders are deeply concerned about making things fair and showing respect. Fairness and respect are essential to preserving the social fabric and their own relationships of trust. Johansson and his colleagues, for example, realized that while they couldn't buffer people from the reality of competition, they could still show respect. "We had a lot of discussions at Volvo in '98, when business trends were weakening, and we had just introduced 'respect for the individual' and the other values," Johansson said. Laying people off "was a necessary thing to do for business reasons, and so we could not refrain from doing it, because it was necessary to reduce costs." But, he continued, "We said, 'We must dismiss people in a respectful way.' And one demand you can make is that people should be made to understand why they are fired. And in general when it comes to reducing costs—synergies—it's not because someone has acted stupidly. They are falling victim to structural reorganization."

For Fradin, who also confronted the need for layoffs, fairness is an absolutely central principle: "I do think that that sense of fairness is very, very important to an organization." From his perspective, it was critical to treat the frontline worker with just as much respect as a senior executive:

When you're laying off frontline people, in my mind it's a really serious bridge you cross. In my view, when we went through that, a greater percentage of the executive suite had to go, compared to the frontline employees. That reflects fairness and a sense of equity—that the people in the call center are just as important as the people in the executive suite. It is very much more, hey, we're in this together. We're going to do it the right way, and we are going to care about people even if we're making really hard decisions. That fits very well my sense of self, and I can go to sleep at night and not worry, even if we are going through some hard times.

"If you're just some sort of ruthless cost cutter," Fradin observed, "and people perceive you that way, then people will find a way to hurt you that I think you'll never see. I really truly believe that. What goes around in life comes around and bites you back in the rear."

Fradin also highlighted the importance of continuing to focus on the business's future growth, even in the midst of difficult decisions: "People wake up in the morning because they want to go to a job that is fulfilling and that they get excited about. There aren't that many people in the world that I've met who get excited by, oh, I'm doing big layoffs today. They get excited because we've got to find the right growth initiatives for them." As a consequence, he said, "One of the things that we are doing and we're doing quite explicitly, is we're using the financial fix-its and restructurings partially to reward our shareholders, but more so, to find the cash and the earnings to fund our growth initiatives."

The concern for fairness extends beyond how to handle painful outcomes to how to reach difficult decisions. The higher-ambition leaders we spoke to work hard to create fair processes for reaching difficult decisions that often have widespread involvement. Johansson, for example, used the first strategy cycle in the spring of 1998 to surface and resolve the car division strategy. Through this process, for many in the group, the requirement to sell the car division became self-evident, rather than a decision Johansson or the leadership team took unilaterally. As Gyllenhammar experienced just a few years before, the decision could have been devastating and blown the group apart. Instead, this time, as Johansson explained, "It certainly was a heated discussion. It was quite hot around the ears for a while, if I can put it like that, but the heat came from the outside, not from the inside. Internally in the organization, there was awareness of the problem with passenger cars. Following the strategic analysis carried out in the spring of '98, people already knew."

One of the clearest examples of the power of a fair process is the experience of Dick Pettingill at Allina Hospitals & Clinics. In 2003, Allina comprised fifteen acute care hospitals and forty-two clinics. Historically, a local board had governed each of the hospitals. But Pettingill, then only twelve months into his tenure as CEO, became convinced that the governance structure was too unwieldy to achieve the required improvements in patient safety, clinical quality, and efficiency, because many of them depended on greater cross-hospital consistency and standardization of practice.

Rather than moving directly to make the changes, however, Pettingill engaged all the hospital boards in a "deliberative process," as he described it. "We got in 240 trustees over a four-month period to come together to be educated both as to how other organizations are governed and what models of governance may or may not apply to our organization." While he hoped for consensus, Pettingill made clear that they would make a decision at the end of the four-month period. In the end, even though they did not get to a consensus, "people felt they had had their day in court and their voice was heard." As a result, when Allina announced in June 2004 that it was consolidating governance under a single, twenty-member board and eliminating the subsidiary boards or reducing them to advisory status. As a result of his strategy, Pettingill recalled, "with the exception of one person, all the previous trustees supported the decision. They may not have agreed with it, but because of the process we went through, they could support the decision."

"When dealing with these tough issues," Pettingill summarized, "it's as much about how you manage the process as the outcome of the decision. You may arrive at a good decision, but if you don't have a good process for getting there, you'll spend the next several years trying to defend the decision."

Clarity: Keep It Simple

The first two principles we have discussed are fundamentally about earning and sustaining the right to lead, about establishing the leader's moral authority, and about building genuine followership. The third principle is about how higher-ambition leaders create an empowering context in which people understand as clearly as possible what matters and what is expected of them.

In earlier research, we found that organizations undergoing major changes commonly suffer from too many and conflicting priorities.[2] In our conversations with higher-ambition leaders, we were struck by their determination and skill in avoiding this trap. Relative to other leaders we have observed or studied, we found that higher-ambition leaders go to extraordinary lengths to keep it simple: to provide clear direction, to distill their agenda to focused priorities, and to keep people focused on productive collaboration rather than organizational complexity. There is an interesting paradox here. Higher-ambition leaders are smart, integrative thinkers, but they use their intellect to try to keep things as simple as possible for the organization—to find the simplicity on the other side of complexity.

From very early on, these leaders find a way to distill their sense of the company's direction into a few simple themes. When Johansson was taking over, for example, and knew he needed to highlight a strategic shift away from Volvo's previous highly divisionalized approach, he focused on the word *shared*. "I started talking about unification, being a group, about culture, shared business ideas, synergies, finding power in each other, a shared technology basis, shared marketing base. The word *shared* was probably the word most frequently used," he said.

Two years later, when integrating Volvo, Renault, and Mack, and consolidating operations, Johansson again found a simple theme to guide the organization: "I have these three Cs that I have stressed a great deal. We are *colleagues,* we work for our *customers,* and then we keep an eye on what our *competitors* are doing. Those are the three Cs that I keep stressing."

This simple formula was Johansson's way of maintaining Volvo's focus on the critical few things that mattered. He realized as he drove Volvo through massive change and restructuring that it would be all too easy for managers to become internally focused and lose sight of the fundamental imperative to serve customers and stay ahead of competitors. For Johansson, the focus on colleagues made explicit a primary source of Volvo's competitive advantage: high-quality collaboration. "No matter what, we are all colleagues," he said, "whether we happen to be a French colleague, a Swedish colleague, or an American colleague, that doesn't really matter. This is something that I try to promote very strongly, so strongly that sometimes other people perceive it as unrealistic. I have tried to be very unambiguous in that respect." In particular, in his experience, that is the way to handle acquisitions: "Inviting everybody to be a colleague on an equal footing."

Johansson emphasized that the distillation of ideas into a powerful communication is a matter of applying the leader's intellect to simplifying. He shared his hard-won experience: "Three words are better than five words and much better than a memo." He goes to considerable lengths to find the right words, ones that will convey the proper emotional meaning. "I am sensitive about words and meanings," he explained, "You have to be careful about the language you choose."

Nestlé's Paul Bulcke highlighted why distilling strategy to a simple theme is so essential: "Alignment is linked with ideas and strategies that are formulated in a clear and simple way. You cannot align people behind something you have to take hours to explain. And as complex as the world may be, you must express your ideas and intentions in simple terms. If you cannot put it into one phrase, you're out. You're out of business in an organization. We want it to be very simple."

When we asked Ollila about the most important thing he had learned as CEO of Nokia, he leaned back and went silent for what seemed like an eternity. Then he looked up and explained that it was about communication—that he had needed to learn how to stay simple in his messages.

This quest for a simple, powerful theme as the basis for aligning the organization, and energizing and guiding its development, is behind the hard work that we described in chapter 3—going beyond complex strategies to a sense of strategic identity. For Ollila and his colleagues at Nokia, as we saw, the theme of "Connecting People" embodied a whole set of meanings about targeting the mass market and developing countries. Similarly, becoming the "best international bank" took on a great depth of meaning at SCB, as distilled in the 140 words of the "Leading the Way" document.

Fradin was able to capture the essence of Hewitt's strategy in the phrase "recentering the business." "I used a phrase over and over again with a lot of our people that we are going through a process where we are 'recentering' the business," he explained. It said that the core of Hewitt's business remained healthy and was a reaction to what Fradin had observed was a preoccupation with the struggles of the outsourcing business: "When I came in, the benefits business and the consulting business had been pretty much ignored while this whole drama was playing out." Fradin used the phrase as a reaffirmation that future prospects were also healthy. "The reason I used that phrase is that the core of the business is being the world's thought leader on human resource and people management issues and how one administers the work that goes along with the management of those people. The recentering of the business is saying that we really do what we do really well, and the even better news is the world really wants it. We just haven't capitalized on it," Fradin said.

A second aspect of keeping it simple that we heard from the higher-ambition leaders is discipline about keeping priorities focused. Tim Solso at Cummins shared his hard-won experience on the importance of maintaining clear and focused priorities: "I have very little patience. I want to get things done fast. So, during my whole career, I would have a long list of things that people should do and I would follow up on it. But a lot of things never got done, because there was no focus." He continued, "I had a very tough time accepting this whole concept of less is more. I just finally learned, if you pick one or two things, and drive it for four or five years, good things will happen."

Ollila made a similar observation: "Jack Welch has about one idea per year that he wants to impose on his organization. He has more ideas, but that's not what you can do. If you reduce it to the bare bones, it must be extremely simple, because otherwise it never reaches the factory in China. It has to reach and sink in, at least to some degree, before you establish the next theme in the organization." The hard work of leadership is the judgment about selecting those priorities. Ollila described the insight required into the organization and what will unlock performance: "You might have your next year's theme, if you understand the deep inside. And to get there, from the detail to the big themes that then move the organization, that's the amazing job."

Higher-ambition leaders are very aware of the risks of getting lost in the complexity of large organizations. The emphasis on keeping it simple is a counterweight to the inevitable tendency in large organizations for things to get complicated. Johansson explained,

It's very easy to lose your way in complexities. When talking about organizational structures, people will always perceive them as very complex. And then I say, "I don't see why it has to be so complex at all. In which way is it complex?" It's not because I don't realize that it is complex, but because if I start declaring that it is complex, it bloody well will be.

You shouldn't think you can change things by means of structures and organizational measures and drawing up tree diagrams and what have you. Most of the problems that emerge and end up on my desk would not be solved by changing the organizational structure of the group. They will be solved by sending twenty-five engineers to the United States. We'll solve it next quarter. We'll solve it quickly, and if you do that systematically you teach an organization the following: Now let's concentrate on the problem instead of chasing internal organigrams and tree diagrams.

By keeping it simple, ensuring that the focus is on the shared objective to be achieved, not differences in culture or organizational position, Johansson helped Volvo set a pace of rationalization that major competitors, such as DaimlerChrysler, could not match.

Persistence: Stay the Course

We have seen throughout this book that achieving a higher ambition requires dogged determination. For Johansson, developing the superiority of Volvo's engine platforms has been a decade-long effort that has involved "extensive initiatives, masses of people, changes in organization structure, changes in product structures, changes in product development structures." Beyond the initial rationalization process over five years from eighteen down to two engine families, the work has been ongoing. When Volvo acquired Nissan Diesel, for example, it was taking on board a whole new engine family, initiating another cycle to "harmonize it with what we have already," said Johansson. Throughout, he has maintained his emphasis on the three Cs, keeping the organization focused on the importance of collaborating with colleagues, and the imperatives driven by customers and competitors.

Maintaining focus and consistency over time allows messages to penetrate sufficiently so that people across the organization understand deeply what is important. Stable, well-understood priorities enable down-the-line leadership and initiative. As Johansson explained, "It is good to give a presentation well, but the most important thing about that presentation is not that the presentation is wonderful; the important thing is that you make it three thousand times."

"You have to bore yourself to death really," Val Gooding, of BUPA, told us. "You have to keep repeating yourself. It is incredibly boring for me to keep saying, 'What matters around here is the customer. The customer is the most important thing.' I've said it hundreds and hundreds and hundreds of times. But it is the reinforcement and continuity of direction and the rearticulation of the goals of the business which is the real job of the CEO, isn't it?"

Staying the course is more than just maintaining a consistent framework and high-level business plan. The stories we heard from the higher-ambition CEOs often highlighted their role in maintaining a consistent direction, even in the face of extreme conflict among stakeholders, and a willingness to follow through on difficult decisions. Johansson described the importance of both vigorous debate and then decisiveness: "I'm fairly tough. I think frank discussions are great, they can be as frank as you like, but once the decision has been made, you bloody have to do what's been agreed and get things done. So it isn't just a matter of saying, 'Okay, I see what you mean. I don't intend to do what you say, but I still want to stay on.' That won't wash with me. I think it's alright to argue with me, and people are happy to do that. However, once the decision has been taken, then we have to push this button and things are now running. And that's what cost us a few managers here."

These CEOs also demonstrate a personal commitment to making sure things get done. As Johansson put it, "When it comes to following up such matters, I'm very much an engineer. Managers call me 'tiresomely bloody structured.' Much of what we do is follow-up activities. We should figure out what we are to do, and then follow it up, making sure that it is in fact done. And if you don't have a follow-up procedure, and you are just sitting there twiddling your thumbs, then things can easily slide." For him, it is about results, not control: "I don't have a strong control reflex. But I do have a strong need for following up and a strong need for achieving results. I want to know how things went."

Fradin similarly highlighted the importance of sustained follow-through. "The vast majority of our challenges are internal as opposed to external, meaning the market demand is there. We need a greater degree of change than we've seen in the past. That's the thing that keeps me up the most, about how do you get that change. Both Hewitt and midwesterners in general are famous for passive-aggressive behavior. You get a lot of head nodding and then nothing really happens after the meeting. I find myself continually having to follow up on items, to double-check."

Ultimately, staying the course is about the leader's own personal commitment. Carl Bennet, former CEO and owner of Getinge, spoke of the importance of commitment. When Bennet bought Getinge in a spin-off from Electrolux in 1993, he came extremely close to bankruptcy before the company turned around. He told us, "I believe that people look for things like long-term endurance." His perseverance has paid off: Getinge has grown to become a $3 billion global leader in its health-care products markets. Bennet said that commitment cannot, under any circumstances, be abandoned simply because things get tough. "I play for the team, even when we have the wind against us," he told us. "In this group, we experience very difficult situations with different product segments which we need to cast off in the longer term. And that is, of course, quite tough, but even when the wind blows hard, I'll still be there. I believe that people see that and don't ever feel that they've been left in the lurch by me. I stay lashed to the mast."

Conclusion

Higher-ambition leaders unleash and channel extraordinary levels of energy by tapping into the higher ambition of people throughout the organization. To do this, however, requires that these leaders develop an integrated solution to a multidimensional set of tasks with a relentlessness and commitment that is the essence of *sisu*.

First, they need to keep finding ways to advance on each of the dimensions we have previously described, working on strategy, performance, and culture simultaneously. It is striking, for example, that Johansson used his first three initiatives as CEO to target each of these dimensions. Thus, he used the tax initiative, in part, to reset performance expectations; he used the values initiative to do the foundation work for building a sense of community, not only across the existing Volvo organization, but also with potential future organizations that might join; and he used the strategy process to surface and address fundamental questions of Volvo's evolving strategic identity.

A second part of the leaders' integrative challenge is that they need to keep working to meet the needs of all key stakeholders, continuing to build trust, alignment on shared purpose, and a shared set of objectives.

The four guiding principles we have described in this chapter—presence, fairness, clarity, and persistence—are ways of enlisting people in doing this work. Leaders who are able to successfully engage and earn trust, make it fair, keep it simple, and stay the course create widespread followership and give people the context and focus to empower their own initiatives.

Doing all these things, however, is not easy, particularly in the face of inevitable setbacks and uncontrollable or unforeseen shifts in the competitive environment. But these leaders understand that they do not have to shoulder this weight alone. We found that higher-ambition CEOs are distinctive in the focus, commitment, and skill with which they develop and unleash collective leadership throughout their firms. This is the subject of the next chapter.

TABLE 6-1

Sisu leadership

	HIGHER-AMBITION LEADERS' APPROACH	
Common leadership pattern	Management "best practices"	Additional distinctive practices
PRESENCE: ENGAGE AND EARN TRUST		
• CEO communications are tightly scripted and controlled • There are few channels for direct, two-way dialogue between managers and lower levels	• Leader spends considerable time and energy directly engaging with people through a wide range of face-to-face, digital, and other communications media	• Leader uses informal forums to create open, two-way communication and build trust • Leader uses open dialogue to learn about self and organization • Leader minimizes differences in formal status and is open to admitting mistakes
FAIRNESS: ESTABLISH A JUST PROCESS		
• Sacrifices not shared equally—lower-level employees disproportionately affected by layoffs, restructuring, and reductions in pay • Senior leaders make important decisions with limited input or engagement from others	• The leader does not shy away from tough decisions about layoffs and restructuring • Leader ensures those hurt by such decisions are treated with dignity and respect • Senior leaders make fair, merit- and fact-based decisions based on best available data	• The pain of organizational change is shared as fairly and equally as possible across all levels • Layoffs are last resort in tough times • Key stakeholders are extensively involved in making difficult decisions • Transparency emphasized to increase trustworthiness of change processes
CLARITY: KEEP IT SIMPLE		
• Strategy has not been distilled into a simple, clear, and easily communicated message	• Strategic and operational direction is distilled into a few simple, easily understandable themes	• Cut through organizational complexities with sharp focus on getting the right people together addressing the right issues

	HIGHER-AMBITION LEADERS' APPROACH	
Common leadership pattern	**Management "best practices"**	**Additional distinctive practices**
• Logic connecting firm strategy and priorities is not well understood • Multiple functional and business priorities have not been reconciled, leading to conflict and overload	• Strong focus on a few strategic priorities • Clear and focused priorities guide and encourage local initiative and entrepreneurship	
PERSISTENCE: STAY THE COURSE		
• The strategic focus shifts regularly in response to changing internal or external conditions or demands • Senior leaders significantly underestimate the time, effort, and repetition required to communicate the company's direction and strategic priorities	• Leaders spend a lot of time communicating • Leadership stays on message and reinforces the key priorities	• Leaders maintain focus and invest over many years in building distinctive capabilities

7

Committing to Collective Leadership

We have so many opportunities, so many problems to solve. The single biggest constraint is who's going to pick up that ball and run with it. And not just do what they're told, but be able to problem-solve in real time, make decisions, and accept account- ability. If I can work out how to accelerate the development of lead- ership capacity by making existing leaders better and attracting more, then all the other problems will solve themselves.

—Peter Sands,
Standard Chartered Bank

BUILDING COMPANIES THAT SEEK to create both eco- nomic and social value is, as we have seen, leadership-intensive. Higher-ambition leaders expect more of themselves, their col- leagues, and their companies. They develop strategies that require outper- formance on key organizational capabilities. They create organizations that can deliver high performance on multiple dimensions but demand a greater capacity to manage internal conflicts and tensions. They dramati- cally raise performance expectations for the delivery of both economic and social value. They unite diverse constituencies into a global community around a shared purpose and common values. We have seen throughout this book that when higher-ambition leaders are able to achieve a "simultaneous solve" on these multiple dimensions, the results can be extraordinary. But achieving this isn't easy, and higher-ambition leaders realize that they cannot do it alone.

In this chapter, we'll look at what makes it possible for these leaders to sustain the intense effort of building exceptional companies: collective leadership. They invest a disproportionate amount of their time in forming an aligned core team at the top and in developing an extended group that can provide distributed leadership across the organization, both now and into the future. Though they themselves are strong individuals, they use their strengths to develop their own teams and hundreds of other leaders, who, in turn, build a culture of commitment and performance throughout the company.

To build such a leadership system, higher-ambition leaders:

- Build a true team at the top.

- Align down-the-line leadership.

- Drive career development.

- Develop next-generation leadership.

Val Gooding's experience and approach to collective leadership is particularly instructive. Over the twelve years from her arrival at BUPA in 1996 to her retirement in 2008, she led a remarkable transformation of both the economic performance and the social institution. Gooding oversaw a rise in revenues from £1 billion to more than £5 billion, and she and her team worked to reconfigure the business portfolio. When she arrived, BUPA was a provider of health insurance and owner and operator of hospitals, with most of its revenue coming from the United Kingdom.

When Gooding departed, BUPA had sold its hospitals, positioned itself in several growth segments of the health market, and generated 50 percent of its revenues from overseas markets.

When BUPA recruited Gooding as managing director for its U.K. business, the core health insurance business was in a perilous state. BUPA was losing market share, and the company's profits had been dropping. Gooding suggested, with a bit of humor, that she might not have taken the job had she realized that the organization was in such a mess. As noted earlier, she acknowledged: "I probably should have done more research. The core business wasn't making any money. The customer service was poor. In my first few weeks, three or four of the senior managers came in and said, 'Oh, we're glad you've come because this will need sorting out. And oh, by the way, if you can't sort it out, we're all leaving.'"

The organization could not continue as it was; it simply would not have had the resources to sustain its operations. Yet, BUPA is an unusual organization: it is a provident association with no shareholders (BUPA stands for British United Provident Association). Any profits are reinvested in the business. So, because there were no shareholders to protest, the deteriorating finances did not bring corresponding external pressures to improve results. There was no "burning platform" from the threat of takeover that might have provoked a turnaround, as it would, for example, in a publicly owned company. BUPA's employees were not even particularly sure that profits really mattered to the organization. As Gooding characterized it, "if you had asked people in BUPA, 'Do we have to make a profit?' you would have gotten a hundred different answers."

To make any change in the business, therefore, and to rescue it from almost certain extinction, leadership had to provide both the urgency and the direction needed to get people engaged and in gear. Gooding and her team had to help forty-five thousand people throughout the organization understand the urgency of improved financial performance and customer service. To do so—in an effort of several years—they did a number of things to sharpen the company's focus on performance, both financial and operational. They created more rigorous financial accountability at all levels of management. They instituted an incentive scheme that gave employees a financial stake in the performance of the business. They invested in IT systems and other tools to improve the ability of frontline call-center workers to deliver superior customer service. They put in place measures of customer satisfaction in every part of the business and set targets and rewarded based on those targets. "Our model is that if we do a good job for our customers, they will recommend us to others, and they will become our advocates," Gooding said. "It will become a circle, and so we will be able to deliver reasonable returns on the investments in our assets. And then we will be able to grow and deliver more health care to more people."

But what was most distinctive was the extent to which Gooding galvanized the turnaround by seeking to change the culture: she invested in leadership and personally modeled the new leadership behaviors. She sought to instill a performance ethic and a customer service orientation, not just by the new metrics and systems, but by drawing out the best in people and tapping their own higher aspirations. Gooding told us: "In terms of changing the culture, I had the chance to do everything I believe in. Either they work or not. That is the joy of being a chief executive. Fortunately, they did work." She was quick to point out, however, that the approach depended on high-quality leadership throughout the organization: "This is just all so big and complicated. My key thing in the success of BUPA is that I have a great team."

It's not that Gooding actually had a great team when she arrived. As we've noted, a good number of them were ready to bolt. Gooding made it a priority to assemble a high-quality senior team and, further, to personally invest the time and energy in creating healthy relationships and building the trust needed for a cohesive, effective team. Gooding also made a major commitment to creating alignment, developing capabilities, and building commitment within the extended leadership group.

In her level of commitment to building collective leadership at both these levels, she was typical of most of our higher-ambition leaders.

Build a True Team at the Top

Creating a high-performing leadership team at the top is hard. In our experience, most senior leadership "teams" are anything but. Often they operate on a hub-and-spokes model, with each team member feeling accountable to the CEO rather than to the team as a whole. Meetings are primarily for information sharing, rather than for collective problem solving and decision making.

The higher-ambition leaders we spoke with took this challenge head on. They set high expectations for their leadership teams, both in creating shared commitment to a common purpose and in driving joint accountability for the performance of the whole rather than just for each member's area of responsibility. They realized that the investment they make in building collective leadership at the top has a dramatic payoff in better strategic decision making and higher levels of teamwork throughout their firms.

"A Lot Smarter Together"

Dale Morrison, CEO of McCain Foods, the world's largest producer of French fries, described a defining moment in an early meeting of the global leadership team. "We got talking about the team, and our CFO said, 'You know, this is not a decision-making body. This is a communications forum where we just exchange information.'" Morrison's immediate reaction was, "Not on my watch!" He made it clear that "we are going to be a lot smarter together. It's not my decision; it's a decision by all of us. We have two hats: the small hat and the big hat." The small hat, Morrison explained, is for each leader's own responsibilities, while "the big hat is really about running this company. We all have to agree on the decisions that we take and be unanimous when we leave the room. We can have conflict within the room, and I hope we do, because then it will be constructive and creative." This moment, as Morrison reflected, reshaped the team's ability to manage a global matrix. The top team could be clear when it was time for the regional presidents to take a step back, take off the small hat, and put on the big hat, because there were global advantages to be gained.

Gary Kelly, CEO of Southwest Airlines, also spoke of the importance of creating a real team at the top: "I am very focused on the team. I don't feel it's about me at all. I feel that we need to have a strong core of officers that work well together and that feel like they are making a major contribution to Southwest Airlines."

Higher-ambition CEOs viewed a well-functioning leadership team as an amplifier, multiplying their reach by an order of magnitude. As Campbell's Doug Conant put it, "you're not in every room and every meeting. So you have to quickly build a team of people that can stand for your value system and subscribe to your way of operating."

They also conveyed a deep conviction in the power of the team as a complement to their own strengths and weaknesses. Gooding noted, for example, "When doing these top jobs, you don't have the complete range of corporate knowledge and capabilities. You try to plug the gaps in your own knowledge and competency base by having really great people that you can trust 100 percent."

Often, the CEOs spoke specifically of a complementary individual, a close associate in the senior leadership team, with whom they formed a more intense partnership. At Bang & Olufsen, for example, CEO Torben Ballegaard Sørensen described how much he valued his relationship with his group co-CEO, Peter Taastrup: "Whereas I'm very development oriented, he is very system and structure oriented, so to this very day, we complement each other well." Similarly, we have seen at Standard Chartered Bank how Mervyn Davies and Peter Sands formed an effective duo. Many of the leaders we met had such an arrangement, one person who had complementary background or skills and with whom they were able to develop and test ideas before going public. Interestingly, at the same time, they were cautious about letting this grow into friendship or favoritism (more about this later). They were careful to focus on the team as a whole and avoid having their judgment biased by losing distance.

The CEOs also depended on the senior team to play a critical integrating role. As we have seen, many were pursuing strategies that put high demands on the ability to set priorities, resolve conflicts, and ensure effective coordination across lines of business, geographies, or functions. They viewed the senior team's effectiveness as a critical determinant of performance in how well their matrix organizations functioned.

Moving Beyond "Politics and Backbiting"

Despite the importance of high-functioning top teams, they are not easy to create. Gooding observed, "A lot of organizations are riven with politics and backbiting and competing and trashing each other." Doug Stotlar made a similar observation about the situation before he took over as CEO of Con-Way, a U.S. transportation company: "I'd observed from my positions below the CEO level, from a business unit perspective, that we were a dysfunctional corporation, with way too much politics at the corporate level."

To overcome this kind of political divisiveness, higher-ambition CEOs had to invest themselves personally in creating healthy relationships and trust. Stotlar explained his approach: "Everybody on the team has to be doing what they do for the right reasons because rogue, independent players with big egos just don't fit here."

Gooding was typical in stressing her personal management style: "I'm very direct. There aren't really hidden agendas around here. If I don't like something, I tend to say, 'I wish you wouldn't do that,' or 'I don't like that,' or 'don't do that' or whatever."

At BUPA, beyond the normal conflicts within a senior team between the lines of business and the functions, there was an extra source of potential conflict: the health insurance business was the largest customer for the hospitals business; hence, one division's cost was another division's revenue. Gooding used her directness to resolve conflicts within the team so that they did not fester or escalate. When there was an issue involving different business divisions or if things were just not going well, Gooding would "get both people in and we would have it all out." She also made explicit her expectations for mutual support and collaboration among the senior team: "If I had two people who would have friction points, I'd say very directly to each of them individually, 'I absolutely expect you to have a great relationship with X. You are not to fall out. You are to be role models for your team of a couple of really supportive colleagues who get along together, who are determined to solve the problem, however difficult it is. And, if possible, I don't want those problems to come to me.'"

Gooding contrasted this direct style with another organization where she had worked: "It was a hugely political place, and everybody was politicking there. The chief executive would never dream of having two people in and saying, 'Look, I know it's really difficult, but I really want you to do this.' He just didn't manage that way. An awful lot of these very, very senior executive issues are tricky and complicated, but sometimes they can be sorted out quite easily by just being very open."

In addition to being direct, Gooding also established an environment in which people expected and encouraged personal feedback from peers and subordinates. She instituted a 360-degree feedback process that extended to the top team, including herself. After her direct reports had filled in a questionnaire about her performance as a leader, she sought additional feedback from colleagues, both because she wanted it and because she wanted to model that behavior for the rest of her team. Gooding remarked, "I said to them, 'Okay, this is what you've all said about me'—I couldn't see their individual scores—'Now you tell me what I can do to do better.'" Gooding explained why she felt this was so important: "There is a natural sort of reluctance to tell the chief executive where she's going wrong. Even if you ask for it and create a space for them to do it, I think some people are just very, very reluctant to do that."

Gooding also emphasized creating an atmosphere of respect. Many other higher-ambition CEOs spoke about the importance of avoiding personal favoritism. Gooding took this one step further than many in emphasizing that there is no "inner clique," that there is no "in" group or "out" group among the senior executives. Ensuring that each executive felt respected and treated equally was sufficiently important to her that she was willing to pay a price to achieve it: "It's much more convenient to have an inner clique, three or four people that you rely on and consult with. My team is about eleven or twelve people. My key colleague is the group finance director. But that's the norm in any company, that the chief executive's closest colleague is going to be the finance director. I consult him hugely. Other than that, there isn't any inner cabinet. There's no inner circle. That's really important for people to feel they've been treated equally."

In addition to directness, personal openness, and respect, Gooding talked about a final dimension in creating the right kind of relationships among the top team: her own personal commitment to them as individuals. She shared her experience with a previous employer that had shaped her views, "I can think of a lot of examples of things that happened to me. Something would go wrong for you personally, and nobody cared really, however senior you were." As CEO at BUPA, she felt it was vital to create a very different relationship with her senior executives. Just as she expected all individuals to display their commitment to the success of the organization and to each other, she believed her own role was to support them in a way that demonstrated her commitment to them and their success:

> If something goes wrong for any of my senior executives, I would move heaven and earth to try and put it right for them, even if that takes a lot of my personal time. Because, you see, those are the key people. That's the great team. They're the ones delivering for me. I

can't make the organization successful without them. I have bent over backwards to try and make this a really happy place for my senior team. By happy, I don't mean easy, however, because they're all ambitious people. They have to have challenge and stretch and new stuff to do and growth opportunities. So I don't mean easy, but I do mean happy, fun, being able to be confident that your boss is supportive of you.

Creating Continuity at the Top

We found that one key contributor to building teamwork at the top was being together for a long time. The longevity of their top teams was a striking feature of our higher-ambition leaders. Many of the teams had been together for five years or more. At the time Nathaniel and our colleague Kathleen Valade MacDonald met with Gooding in London in April 2007, Gooding's senior team had been largely intact for about seven years. "That's probably very old-fashioned," she said, "but we benefit from that. If you're together for six, seven, eight years, you can't forget about the mistakes. Actually, the corporate memories that you share are an important part of achieving really good performance."

Bertrand Collomb represented an extreme. He described his years as CEO of Lafarge, world leader in cement and construction materials: "I had pretty much the same team for fifteen years," he said. "It helped me very much. It was a very strong team."

For several of the leaders, including Ed Ludwig at Becton Dickinson and Tim Solso at Cummins, the team had, in effect, risen together as a cohort, a new generation taking on the leadership mantle. At Nokia, for example, when the board made Jorma Ollila the CEO, he brought in a team of likeminded managers from the cellular phone division. "After a year or two," he said, "they became the management team. And they made it all happen."

Ollila managed to keep his team together for the next ten years, as they built Nokia from a Finnish conglomerate to the world's largest cell-phone company. They formed a tightly knit group that provided coherent unified leadership. They deliberately coordinated their behavior to make sure that they were conveying the same messages, even agreeing to tidy up their language: "swearing stops here." Like most of the leaders we spoke with, Ollila made every effort to shift the responsibility for the company's success onto the entire group. "It was a very special setup," he told us. "They were each individually hugely respected" within the group, and together, in Ollila's view, they were the source of Nokia's success. "When I had the first interview internationally, they wanted to do a cover story. I said only on one condition: you will have to highlight the team," said Ollila.

In companies where the CEO was recruited from the outside, the new leader had to assemble the team, typically over the period of two or three years. There was no single model for how the CEOs did this. Some of them were able to fashion a team from players already in place. Russ Fradin, for example, joined Hewitt Associates just shortly after the company had also recruited a new CFO and a new head of administration. Fradin was able to construct a core team with them, together with the leaders of the two businesses that had been most successful. At the other extreme, Campbell's Doug Conant arrived at a business that had been sorely depleted by departures and had to remake an entire team.

At BUPA, Gooding found a leadership of varying quality, from the top management team to managers on lower levels. "There were variable qualities of management. There were really great people but also quite inadequate people. It was a bit directionless, really," Gooding said. Part of the issue was a poor track record with external hires: "People would come in, and within a year they would be paid off and they'd be gone." Gooding found she was able to build her senior team around a number of existing players: "I suppose the mix in my team when I became chief executive was probably about sixty-forty, internal appointments and new people that came in over a period of time."

Maintaining Some Personal Distance

While the higher-ambition CEOs spoke eloquently about the importance of their top team and invested a great deal of emotional energy in building the team's effectiveness, their relationships with the members of the team were, for the most part, purely professional. Lafarge's Collomb was typical. When asked whether he was personal friends with the team, he replied, "No, if you call personal friends people who meet each other outside of work, no. My wife is the very good friend of one of the wives because they both ride horses, and she comes with us on riding trips, but not her husband."

Stefan Persson at H&M, a $20 billion Swedish fashion retailer with stores in 38 countries, described his relationship with one member of his executive team: "Think about how much time we spent working together. We were on business trips several days every week. We had dinner, breakfast, and lunch together. If we had started socializing as friends on top of that, that would have been too much."

Others also remarked that the role required them to maintain a certain distance. They couldn't let themselves get too close; their judgment couldn't become clouded by personal ties that had become too strong. In answer to a question about their greatest challenges as a CEO, many focused on the decisions they had had to make about senior team members. Gooding spoke for many when she said: "Some of the key things have been about the people—hiring and firing. We haven't done a lot of hiring and firing, but when to hold on to somebody and when should they leave? When should a new person come? Who is that person?" Those decisions, already difficult, can become agonizing when personal friendships are also at stake.

Align Down-the-Line Leadership

The higher-ambition CEOs did not just focus on forging an aligned top team. They also invested heavily in developing an extended leadership group, typically comprising two hundred to five hundred leaders in key positions throughout the organization, into an active partner in realizing the strategic vision for the enterprise. The depth and quality of initiative emanating from this group of leaders, the CEOs believed, was critical to success in mobilizing high levels of commitment and sustained performance from the broader organization. As Standard Chartered Bank's Peter Sands emphasized:

> We have so many opportunities, so many problems to solve. The single biggest constraint is who's going to pick up that ball and run with it. And not just do what they're told, but be able to problem-solve in real time, make decisions, and accept accountability. If I can work out how to accelerate the development of leadership capacity by making existing leaders better and attracting more, then all the other problems will solve themselves.

The major vehicles the CEOs used to reach these leaders are familiar—leadership development programs, career development and placement, and accountability metrics. But we were repeatedly struck by the remarkable levels of time and energy higher-ambition CEOs invested in the strategic use of these vehicles to build a strong cadre of leaders.

Using Leadership Development Programs to Communicate Expectations and Unleash Initiative

Many of the higher-ambition CEOs not only invested significantly financially in professional development programs, but also chose to be personally involved in designing and participating in key aspects of them.

Gooding, for example, galvanized the early stages of the culture change by engaging all the U.K.-based employees in a one-day program that was intended to tap into their own aspirations. "We used that day," she explained, "to articulate our vision of this as all a matter of our customers. But we didn't do it in what I call a 'sheep dip' way. In other words, we didn't say, 'Okay, we're just going to have everybody out for a day, we're going to tell them what it is, and then they're going to go out the other end' and they're left being processed." Instead, Gooding chose a different approach: "We said that making this business successful is about you bringing to it your personal attributes and motivation. So we called the day 'One Life.' It was all about how you've got one life, and you've got things you bring to your life and to your work, and so on. We want to help you maximize the contributions that you're making in your job."

That program then served as the backdrop for a training program for all the managers across the business, reaching about a thousand in total, which sought to instill greater customer focus and raise performance standards. Gooding viewed this as one of the most important methods she had for shaping the culture. She explained:

> The leadership program ran for about eighteen months to two years. I went to every program, so more or less every week I was leaving London on a Thursday afternoon and driving out to Berkshire. I would do a closing session on the program. . . . It's just so incredibly important, when you're trying to do a change program, for people to see the leader of the business giving total commitment to it. And, of course, there is a sort of myth building that goes on that not many people talk about. The fact that I did that for eighteen months, the word gets out. People start to say, "My goodness, that's a huge commitment for her to do that. Why is that so important? My goodness, this must be really important."

Gooding used her personal participation to model new leadership behaviors for inviting feedback and making it discussible. She saw these behaviors as fundamental to the new culture and realized how difficult they would be to shift, so she made it a personal mission: "When I went every time, every week, off to the countryside to talk to these people, I used to take my 360-degree feedback with me. I used to read out the odd good bits so they didn't think I sounded totally incompetent and make them wonder,

'Why have we got her as a chief executive?' But I also used to say, 'Look, this is one of the things that people think I should do better, you see. I need to work on this. I'd make a joke about some of it, and I'd say what I was trying to do about it."

The reason she did that, she explained, was to role model and make the point: "However important you are, you can be straightforward about uncomfortable feedback, and you can ask people to help you with it." After the program, she expected the leaders to take their own 360-feedback back to discuss with their teams. Gooding continued, "They wouldn't necessarily say to their teams, 'Oh, Val Gooding said this.' I'm sure they didn't. But they remembered how I had done it. So they could think, 'Oh, she could do that with us; surely, I can do it with my team.'"

Role modeling, for Gooding, is not limited to the leadership programs themselves. She remarked, "Because we're a service business, it's absolutely vital that the senior managers are visible in the frontline of the business with the customers and patients and residents in our care. So, from the very beginning, I spent time in the call centers, in the hospitals."

Gooding's purpose in making those visits was in part to communicate expectations to her managers. "I still go a lot to hospitals and nursing homes and call centers. In particular, I sit with the people in our call centers, and I listen to calls. I've always done that. Of course, it's incredibly useful because then you find out what the customers are saying. But more than that, it's all about this building of an idea about what's important around here," she said. She was getting people to think, "If it's important enough for the chief executive to come and sit with Maisie and listen to the calls, that must be a really important thing, because why would she keep doing it? Obviously, if I do it, my direct reports are more likely to follow suit and do it as well."

Anders Dahlvig and his top-team colleagues at IKEA spent several days in every high-level leadership development program, both to contribute to the learning sessions and also as an opportunity to monitor and assess the leadership pipeline. At Nestlé, Paul Bulcke and his team regularly participated in the same types of events, making sure to discuss strategies and values with the managers coming to the training center from all over the world.

Dale Morrison told us that he was particularly proud of the "Leading Growth" workshops he instituted at McCain Foods, together with his chief human resources officer, Janice Wismer. Designed to reach the two hundred leaders most critical to the company's success, the initiative brought them together in groups of fifteen for an intensive three-day session. Each group combined leaders from across business areas, geographies, and functions. "I get goose bumps every time I look at the group list," Morrison told us. "This is our power. We better harness it."

For three uninterrupted days, the fifteen leaders worked with Morrison on personal leadership and the future of the company. On the first day, the participants confronted such general questions as: What is leadership? What does it take to be a good leader? Together they explored these concepts, sharing their own personal experiences and building new levels of understanding and connection with colleagues. On the second day, the group focused on leadership at McCain to understand where there were opportunities for growth and development and how transformation could occur. And on the third day, the participants worked on their individual leadership. "It's a powerful, powerful session," Morrison said. "The power in the session is that we have no outsiders. We learn from each other."

We would add that some of the power in the session also came from the two-way communication that Morrison created with the participants. The sessions were intimate and intense. At one stage, participants could ask Morrison anonymous questions on any topic. The most difficult question for him, Morrison told us, was when he was asked, "If you were to die tomorrow, who would give your eulogy, and what would they say?"

Overall, Morrison characterized these sessions as very important. "We've had people crying," Morrison said. "It is, for many, hugely transformational."

In addition to their direct personal involvement, many of the CEOs ensured that leadership development was tightly integrated with addressing important business issues. At Nordea bank, Christian Clausen selected a dozen young leaders from different geographies and functions to work as an advisory group to the top team, developing proposals on emerging strategic issues.

In a similar vein, Brian Walker told us how Herman Miller has developed a flexible approach that simultaneously develops talent and engages rising leaders in the organization. When the senior management team identifies something they want to explore, investigate, or launch, they put together a small team of developing leaders to take on the problem. They do this three or four times a year.

The program creates an opportunity for the new leaders to tackle more difficult problems and for the management to test them out. Walker emphasized that, "we've had real things come out of them." They have started new businesses on recommendations from these collaborative efforts. For example, one young woman told him that if he ended up taking the proposal forward, she'd like to be put in charge. "She now runs the business," Walker said.

One important element of Walker's approach is the fluidity of his teams. They are put together on a project basis, and team members can come from anywhere in the organization. Once the project is complete, the team is disbanded. This reinforces the company culture and horizontal lines of communication. It allows for a greater diversity of perspectives. And it enables Walker to harness the power of young talent while grooming the next generation of leaders.

Drive Career Development

Higher-ambition leaders also took an unusual level of personal interest in the career development of their extended leadership team, even several layers down in the organization. Ollila, for example, told us: "Look at the management team now, the forty-year-olds. I picked them. I have watched them from when they were below thirty. I know these people." He continued, "I manage through people, so it means I have to know everybody." Carlo Pesenti believed the development of leadership talent in Italcementi's nineteen countries of operations so essential that he chose to view himself as one of the company's two HR directors.

Like Ollila and Pesenti, these CEOs saw their involvement in annual reviews and career planning as one of their most important priorities and were willing to devote the necessary time to it. Leif Johansson, for example, described the process at Volvo: "It ends with me sitting from November to December each year with each business area and each larger business unit and going through how their competence development looks in relation to key recruitment issues. I did not think that it was that important at the beginning, but I have realized that I was wrong. The fact that everyone knows that I sit at a table and go through the five hundred to six hundred highest managers on an individual basis is very important."

In particular, the CEOs spoke of their personal interest in finding people who embody the company's values and culture. Dahlvig described the importance of fit in selection and promotion at IKEA: "We have an instrument that allows employees to provide feedback about their bosses. In principle, every third year, all our employees send in their feedback, a hundred thousand forms in a standardized format in which we ask questions that we think are important for our culture, but also other types of managerial questions." As a consequence, he continued, "We know exactly which managers our employees think are good representatives of the IKEA culture, who work in a serious manner, and who try to develop their ability to manage. We know exactly who they are. That means that we can work with them to develop them or get rid of them."

The CEOs also used career moves and temporary assignments as a way of shaping a network of relationships that would help bind the company together and facilitate collaboration. In chapter 2, Sands spoke about the deliberate rotation of key people across functions and geographies at SCB. As the CEOs described their approaches, they displayed unusual attention to realizing people's potential. "It's often about unlocking people you've got," observed Sands, "working out how to put them in a different place, or help them build on strengths they've got that they haven't quite realized how to use."

In this effort, the CEOs focused not only on what the individual could do for the company. Several emphasized their concern for helping each individual develop to his or her full potential, whether or not that proved to be within the company or elsewhere. This above-and-beyond commitment *to* the individual essentially mirrors the higher commitment these leaders sought *from* the individual: a commitment to the success of the institution beyond pursuit of the individual's direct interests.

The CEOs focused on career development not only to appropriately place individuals but also to establish an overall balance in the development of the company's leadership capacity. Ballegaard Sørensen explained his approach to striking the right balance. Bang & Olufsen has established a model for what it has called *yin-yang* leadership. All managers are categorized as either "action oriented" (X) or "structuralists" (Y). Ballegaard Sørensen told us, "We always make sure that if there is an X up here, we need a Y over there, and if we have a Y over here, we might want to have two Xs over there." To have only action-oriented people in the corporate offices, for example, wouldn't work, he explained. "If things become too rigid and we get too many structuralists, things will grind to a halt," he added. "We need some wildness."

Dahlvig introduced one of the most systematic approaches to developing collective leadership when he became the CEO of IKEA in 1999. IKEA does not hire any new managers above the store manager level. The result is that the upper-level executives have held positions in all ranks of the organization. Dahlvig himself rose through a number of positions, from store manager to country manager and ultimately CEO.

Top executives come to their positions with a real knowledge of IKEA's culture and a well-developed web of relationships across the business. To ensure they continue to cultivate relationships throughout the hierarchy, IKEA holds annual antibureaucracy weeks, during which it requires high-level managers (including the top team) to spend one week on the floor. Dahlvig told us, "It involves our most-senior two thousand executives. We want the people who are heads of purchasing to work out there in the stores, so that they'll be able to understand the consequences of what they do when making their purchases." When Tobias and Flemming interviewed him, Dahlvig had just returned from a week in a warehouse, where he had been responsible for filling the storage shelves with bookshelves and other pieces of furniture.

Because almost all IKEA leaders are hired from within, Dahlvig is invested in fostering leadership within the company. "The IKEA Way" is a cultural training program that occurs on a national and global level. "There is a continuous process of improving, and reinforcing the culture in the leadership, because this is really the most important thing for the managers," Dahlvig said. Along with his top team, he makes his relationship with the top management and the extended network of leaders a priority.

Develop Next-Generation Leadership

The level of investment that many of these CEOs made in developing down-the-line leadership was remarkable. They viewed their investment as critical to successfully achieving their vision for the enterprise. For many, though, the time frame for evaluating the payback of that investment was very long-term. They viewed themselves as developing the next generation of leaders that would be critical to securing the long-run future.

Some of the CEOs who were well along in their tenure were focused specifically on the leaders who would form the next generation of top leaders. At Cummins, for example, Solso told us, "A year and half ago, realizing I'm getting near the time to retire at sixty-five, we identified the next generation of leadership—eighteen people." Solso described the level of effort the company has made in developing them as a group: "We put together a two-and-a-half-year program where once every other month, six times a year, they get together. And they have to come. It's a day and a half in most cases. But we've taken those groups to China; we've taken them as a group to India. So they learn our businesses, they learn the culture, they learn what's going on, and they learn it together."

Solso designed the program by asking himself, "What are all the things that I had no exposure to before I became CEO that I wish I would have had?" He elaborated: "We've taken them to Washington, D.C., to see how government relations work. We've taken on such topics as energy, oil, Islam, terrorism. We've taken them to Wall Street to see how the capital markets work. They're spending two sessions on diversity and one on leadership." Solso envisioned that the outcome would be well worth the investment: "After two and half years, first, they will have developed close working relationships, which is important if they are going to lead later on. Second, they've had some exposure to things they wouldn't normally see."

Conant developed a similarly targeted program at Campbell's: "I'm cultivating the next generation of leaders myself in a hands-on way." He personally worked with twenty-five individuals over the course of two years. "I'm trying to help them each build a personal leadership philosophy," he said. "Not necessarily mine, but something that works for them."

Other CEOs were more focused on meeting the long-term strategic requirements for leadership. Johansson stressed the importance of recognizing that the environment of major corporations is becoming truly global. In Volvo's case, its business-to-business customers are demanding global offers and services. Accordingly, Johansson has already reshaped the board from being all Swedish to including Chinese, French, Indian, and U.S. members, and established a principle that management teams of each division should be similarly cosmopolitan. This, in turn, has given urgency to developing young talent from across the far-flung network of Volvo's operations.

Johansson expressed a sentiment many other of our CEOs shared: "Volvo has a soul as a company that I have been able to join and be a part of developing. But this soul doesn't end with me; it will pass to the next generation and be made to work well. One of my tasks is to make sure that the company will continue to exist in the longer term." He continued, "No matter what, I intend to leave behind a Volvo that does have a soul that can march on under a new leadership."

To Gooding, leadership development was vital not just for securing the future of the institution, but as perhaps her most important legacy: "Part of one's legacy is having done enough that inspires and encourages business careers to develop and grow. If you have really led a company exceptionally well and you've done unique and different things that inspired people, who remember those things for a long time, and then when they're faced with a difficult set of circumstances or a management challenge, they think, 'Well, what would Val Gooding have done about? She used to do it this way.'" For Gooding, her most significant legacy is how her individual leadership contribution "resonates with people and how it helps them in their jobs and careers in the future."

Conclusion

The commitment to collective leadership we have described in this chapter is one of the most significant differentiators between the success and failure of higher-ambition leaders. We are familiar with several leaders with high aspirations who have fallen short because they did not develop the collective leadership capacity required to sustain their strategy and simultaneously address their multiple challenges.

Investment in collective leadership capacity is rarely the most urgent matter on the CEO's desk. There are always pressing and competing demands for resources and for the CEO's time. Yet there are powerful forces that insidiously undermine leadership effectiveness. Even within the best-intentioned senior team, the stresses and dynamics of rapid change will lead to conflicting priorities and undermine coordination. Similarly, even among the most idealistic leaders in the extended leadership group, inevitable breakdowns in communication across departments, lack of clarity on objectives, or integrity gaps between leadership's vision and actions can quickly breed cynicism, a loss of commitment, and a descent to expedience.

To keep these forces in check and to build and sustain aligned leadership, the CEOs in our sample bring unwavering focus and a commitment to ongoing learning—for themselves, the senior team, and down-the-line leaders. Once they have formed their senior team, they tend to keep it relatively intact over time and consciously drive out politics by inviting feedback; they also model the need for honesty and openness in the wider leadership group to create a culture of learning how to lead. Beyond traditional succession planning, they invest in building the next generation of leaders, aware that just as organizations never reach an ideal or finished state, leadership capabilities must always be renewed to face upcoming challenges.

TABLE 7-1

Committing to collective leadership

	HIGHER-AMBITION LEADERS' APPROACH	
Common leadership pattern	**Management "best practices"**	**Additional distinctive practices**
BUILD A TRUE TEAM AT THE TOP		
• Leadership team functions primarily as information-sharing body • Team members are held accountable to the CEO, but not to each other • Political jockeying and competition among members are common	• Leadership team sets priorities and resolves conflicts collectively • Effective teamwork primarily through structured formal meetings • Interpersonal relationships are good	• There is a sense of shared responsibility and passion for the overall success of the enterprise • Team members maintain deep, trust-based relationships for many years • Certain team members play specific and complementary leadership roles to the CEO in the overall management of the enterprise
ALIGN DOWN-THE-LINE LEADERS		
• Formal training programs and periodic annual meetings are held for the extended leadership group	• CEO shares information and solicits feedback on key issues in company meetings • CEO engages down-the-line leaders in dialogue about company values and expected behavior	• CEO designs and teaches leadership development programs • CEO takes personal risks by revealing personal experiences that shaped values and assumptions
DRIVE CAREER DEVELOPMENT		
• Career development is largely controlled by local managers • There is little visibility and sharing of talent across the business	• Strong formal systems for managing the talent pipeline • High-potential people are identified and supported • Career and professional development plans are established for key managers	• The CEO takes direct personal interest in development of several hundred down-the-line leaders • Talent reviews involve managers from different parts of organization to calibrate standards and ensure mobility • Company leaders are teachers in company management development programs

	HIGHER-AMBITION LEADERS' APPROACH	
Common leadership pattern	**Management "best practices"**	**Additional distinctive practices**
DEVELOP NEXT-GENERATION LEADERSHIP		
• The primary focus is on filling current openings with the best available talent, internally or externally	• The company has a good succession planning process • The management bench is strong and deep	• CEO personally mentors leaders on threshold of joining senior team • Next-generation leaders are explicitly deployed to drive strategic change • Potential senior leadership successors sought with backgrounds, perspectives, and capabilities that are key for the firm's future success, even if those capabilities are quite different from those of current leadership

Part Three

Moving to a Higher Ambition

Becoming a Higher-Ambition Leader

The ability to lead and inspire others stems directly—and I mean
directly—from the ability to lead and energize and inspire myself.
In those moments when I am crystal-clear about what I stand for,
and what I'm doing, and why I'm doing it, and why it matters, I can
talk to anybody and get them fired up.

—Peter Dunn,
former CEO of Steak 'n Shake

W E HOPE THAT THE examples of the CEOs portrayed in this book will help raise the level of your own leadership ambitions. It is hard to imagine a more energizing, meaningful way to spend your professional life than to play a central leadership role in building a higher-ambition company. But this work is far from easy, as should be clear by now. As Doug Conant suggested, higher-ambition leaders must earn the right to lead. Success requires a mastery of not just the hard disciplines of business—strategy, financial analysis, operations, marketing—but intangibles, including the capacities to see yourself and your organization with a clear eye, to unleash the latent capabilities in others, and to lead from values and purpose.

Most of all, higher-ambition leadership requires an extraordinary level of personal *integrity*. By integrity, we mean something that includes, but goes beyond, honesty and ethics. The leaders in our sample worked as hard as possible to integrate their decisions and actions with their values and beliefs. Even when engaging in the difficult work of downsizing or restructuring, they did not emotionally distance themselves or abandon their humanity. Higher-ambition leaders are also uniquely skilled at *integrating* actions in different domains of business, from strategy to finance to people; they were always moving to find the "simultaneous solve."

What essential things must managers do to become higher-ambition leaders? In this chapter, we outline the state of mind and heart required. Higher-ambition leaders would counsel you to:

- Find your anchor.

- Choose your teachers well.

- Learn from experience.

- Engage in honest conversations.

Find Your Anchor

Higher-ambition CEOs were able to exercise the *sisu* leadership we describe in chapter 6 by staying anchored. That means they developed a philosophy and personal goals that enabled them to find in their work a larger purpose that could inspire not only themselves, but others. And they relied on family, friends, and trusted colleagues to help them stay centered and maintain their integrity. To keep their integrity, they did not compartmentalize their roles in life, as CEO, spouse, parent, and community member. Flemming and Tobias asked Volvo's Leif Johansson how he coped with the enormous stress during the economic meltdown of 2008 and 2009. He said that he maintained his equilibrium by thinking about his family and friends and how they were more important to him than his job. He came to this realization early in his career, he said, when he was in his first CEO job as head of Electrolux. He felt, as did Nestlé's Paul Bulcke, that if he had to choose between job and family, he would not hesitate: family came first. Also, Johansson used his family for what he termed the "kitchen table test"—running ideas by them—to stay anchored and to ensure that he made difficult decisions with regard to human values. He explained that in order to test a potential course of action, he would ask himself whether he would be comfortable sitting at the kitchen table on a Saturday morning explaining to his wife and children what he had done and why.

Finding your anchor is a process that begins early in your career and requires the courage to discover who you are and to shape yourself into the person, and the leader, you would like to be. Peter Dunn, former CEO of Steak 'n Shake, told us, "If you are not strong enough as a human being to withstand a fair amount of heat, and basically know why you're doing what you are doing, and to energize and inspire yourself in a very grounded way, the odds of your coming out of this alive are almost zero, because it's too hard." Leaders cannot achieve high performance or real commitment to building a social institution, he said, when they "do *not* know who they are and what they are trying to do." The ability to lead and inspire others, he continued, "stems directly—and I mean directly—from the ability to lead and energize and inspire myself. In those moments when I am crystal-clear about what I stand for, and what I'm doing, and why I'm doing it, and why it matters, I can talk to anybody and get them fired up. I have to speak from the heart."

Bill George, former CEO of Medtronic and now a professor who teaches leadership at the Harvard Business School, suggested that to become anchored and learn who you are requires self-awareness: "You can't have self-confidence until you have the self-awareness that can lead to self-acceptance. Those three things are so tightly tied together, it's hard for me to tease them out. That's an extremely important chain for every leader to go through. Those who don't are extremely vulnerable to making bad decisions under pressure."

George noted that self-awareness, in turn, leads to the emotional intelligence that is so essential to successful leadership, especially in large, global institutions. "I've seen dozens, if not hundreds, of leaders fail, and everyone has failed for lack of emotional intelligence," George said. "The key to emotional intelligence is self-awareness. Short of self-awareness, you can keep making the same mistakes over and over and again." George suggested that self-awareness must be developed and needs to be grounded in regular habits and practices. For him, those habits include jogging three or four times a week, meditating twenty minutes twice a day, talking with his wife about important issues, and mentoring and being mentored. Leaders need such practices, so that when they find themselves under extreme pressure, they will be ready to manage the stress and lead with integrity.

Choose Your Teachers Well

Higher-ambition leaders also understand that learning from others and leveraging their strengths is not a sign of weakness, but rather is essential for their development.

Many of the higher-ambition CEOs said that they had had bosses with the right values and practices at critical points in their careers, and they had served as invaluable sources of development. Johansson, who spent the first part of his career at Electrolux as unit head and CEO for a number of subsidiary companies, told us that he had "the good fortune of having had extremely good bosses." Among them was Hans Werthén—a "legendary figure"—who made a comment to Johansson that he has never forgotten and that has "shaped his philosophy of management." Johansson, then thirty-one, had been charged with turning around a troubled subsidiary of the company. After some investigation, Johansson made some harsh observations about the employees in the unit. Werthén listened and then said, "Leif, when you start thinking that half the people around you must be bloody idiots, you need to think about which of the two halves you belong to yourself." Johansson remembers that Werthén was angry with him, which hurt, but the advice was good. "He was just taking me to task," he said.

Many higher-ambition leaders, including George and Conant, looked to mentors and coaches to support their development and talked about the importance of finding the right ones. Mentors can serve almost as a personal board of directors.[1] George suggested that the key to learning from mentors is trust: "You have to know they care about you, before you'll take the advice."

Coaches can help leaders deal with what Allina's Dick Pettingill called "flat spots." He said, "I've always been a strong proponent of executive coaching, of having the sounding board that you can use and consult with and bounce ideas off of in the solitude of the moment. I've always had somebody at my side." He believes that the coach should come from outside the company, so that he or she is not beholden to either the leader or the organization for his or her livelihood.

Higher-ambition CEOs were also adept at learning from members of their own leadership teams. Carl Bennet, who developed a small company, Getinge, into a world leader in its markets, spoke more than once about how the people you have in your team psychologically grow with you and spur your growth as well. He was convinced that you can only be as good as the people you surround yourself with. Christian Clausen frankly told us how he gains strength from joint problem solving with his team at Nordea: "All this uncertainty and worry! Every day, there is a new thing about which I think, 'Oh what's all that about?' But my experience is that, if I'm put together with the right people, I always come up with solutions that are very good."

Many of our leaders said that it's important to identify your weaknesses and find one or more team members whose strengths offset your weak points. For example, in discussing the turnaround they co-led in the 1990s at Asda, the British grocery retailer, Archie Norman and Allan Leighton told Mike Beer that neither of them alone could have turned the company around. As CEO, Norman brought discipline, intellect, and a sure sense of strategy, while Leighton, first hired as marketing director, brought great people skills. As a result of their working relationship, Leighton became more analytical and task-oriented, while Norman got more adept at engaging with people and shaping culture.

Learn from Experience

Many of our CEOs told us that "lessons of experience" were the most powerful source of their development.[2] Some of the higher-ambition leaders, like Paul Bulcke and Ed Ludwig, who spent their entire careers in one company, learned from different assignments within a single organization. Ludwig explained that these built confidence, which is a necessary ingredient for successful leadership. Ludwig grew up in a blue-collar family and was the only one to go to college. He joined Becton Dickinson and, through a number of different roles, ended up as CEO. "There's a little bit of 'My God,'" Ludwig said, "that makes you wonder if you got there by mistake." But along the way, he said, "I grew more confident. I'm willing to express myself a little bit more now. I'm stepping out."

Like Ludwig, many of the CEOs we interviewed did not think of themselves as fully developed when they took on the CEO role. Several told us that the challenging prospect of the job was scary (we heard the phrase "holy shit" more than once in this regard), but that coping with the challenge—experiencing both successes and failures and using those experiences as learning opportunities—enabled them to develop their leadership repertoire.

To add to the complexity of leadership, careers in the twenty-first century are more likely to be protean than in times past. There will be even more twists and turns, a larger number of shifts, possibly higher highs and lower lows. So we recommend that aspiring leaders take charge of their learning by always choosing the job that will challenge their capabilities and demand them to increase their knowledge, refine their values, and develop their leadership capabilities. In this kind of job, they will be forced to figure out how to relate to their team, how to work with them to solve problems, and how to leave behind the idea that the leader has to know all the answers.

Given the importance of learning from the right experiences, the choice of employer is critical. When considering a job, aspiring leaders should determine if the organization and its leaders possess higher-ambition values and believe in a higher purpose. They should evaluate the culture to see if it is one in which performance is assessed rigorously and where only the best succeed. And they should learn what values and principles underlie the culture of the organization. Do those values and principles embody the human values and ethics of higher-ambition companies?

In addition to choosing the right and properly challenging job, higher-ambition leaders also have a remarkable capacity to acknowledge and learn from difficult, even traumatic, experiences. Conant talked candidly about how he got through the experience of being fired from General Mills, after ten years with the company, with the help of coaches and counselors. "I developed a ton of humility around that experience," he said, "and a whole new view of how fortunate I was when I was working. I didn't really appreciate it until I lost it."

Getinge's Bennet remembered a dramatic learning experience that came early in his career, when at Electrolux. He was still in his twenties when the company tapped him to make major changes to a unit based in France. During his first days there, a group of radical union members had hung a doll bearing his name, with a noose around its neck, off the roof of one of the company buildings, "just to show me who was in charge." Bennet had to find the courage to continue undaunted with his assignment, which he completed successfully over the following year and a half.

Recall also Anand Mahindra's encounter with union workers who wanted to throw him from a balcony and the lessons he took from that encounter. Emotionally laden experiences like these can be powerful learning opportunities.

Engage in Honest Conversations

The leaders in our study used many mechanisms—including team-building meetings, various forums, and social media—to help themselves, their teams, and members of the larger organization and surrounding community engage in honest conversations from which they learned to confront reality and find ways to deal with it.

In chapter 4, we saw how Ludwig, when he became CEO of Becton Dickinson, faced up to a problem of his own making: the limping implementation of a $100 million enterprise software system that he had championed and led as CFO. His dramatic mea culpa came about because one of his first acts as CEO was commissioning a task force to interview managers across the globe about BD's strengths and barriers to implementing its strategy. This effort made him see just how badly the execution of the enterprise system was going, something he had been unable to fully face when he was leading the project. He accepted the task force's findings, admitted his role in the failure, and made a commitment to the task force—and later to the entire company—that he would fix it.[3]

At Medtronic, George employed periodic team-building sessions to develop trust and get unvarnished input on how to improve his leadership effectiveness: "Almost from day one, we went offsite for three days once or twice a year. I always used a facilitator because I wanted to be a participant, not the leader, and to give people the opportunity to give me very critical feedback that we could really talk about."

Hewitt's Russ Fradin captured the essence of these learning processes when he told us, "In every forum, you try to listen. You ask others, 'What's on your minds?' 'What would you be worried about if you were me?'" Such forums required leaders to listen and be open to what they heard; they also enabled them to develop their capacity to receive feedback without being defensive—to learn uncomfortable truths about the business, organization, and their leadership without loss of confidence in themselves as leaders—a skill that we find too few leaders possess. Fradin stressed the importance of honest conversations and the benefits of admitting errors. It can be both helpful and cathartic, he said, to look people "in the eye and say 'I was wrong' or 'We made a mistake.' If you're always right, there is no trust. Nobody's that smart."

Conclusion

Higher-ambition CEOs are as concerned about people and the larger good as they are about financial results. They spend time developing trusting relationships with people across many constituencies, creating an emotional bank account they can draw on when times get tough—as they almost certainly will. Yet these relationships are deliberately not intensely personal, because such ties can cloud the decision-making process.

The CEOs in our sample also do psychological work to strengthen themselves as individuals. By looking inward, they become more aware of who they are and of their values and purpose. They often seek coaches and mentors who remind them to reaffirm what they stand for and, when a crisis comes, to keep their eyes on what really matters. These leaders seek to inspire themselves and thereby inspire others.

The most important way our leaders develop is by learning and growing from experience. They find that success offers useful lessons and that failure, if allowed, can be an even more potent teacher. Bosses also make strong teachers. Great learning can occur in open, honest conversations with almost anyone in the company. The education our CEOs cared most about was not the technical and business learning they had gathered, but the deeply personal lessons. All the higher-ambition leaders started early in their careers to work on the "soft stuff" and to develop a clear philosophy of management and leadership that guided them on the path toward achieving their goals.

You may find the following questions useful, as you consider your development as a higher-ambition leader:

FIND YOUR ANCHOR

- Am I anchored in a philosophy of life, family, and work that enables me to find and serve a higher purpose, check my ego, and know what is right?

- Am I developing habits for life and work that will enable me to stay centered so I can make wise decisions?

CHOOSE YOUR TEACHERS WELL

- Do I have leaders from whom I can learn?

- Am I comfortable accepting and using help from others?

LEARN FROM EXPERIENCE

- Do I have a career plan that will provide me with the lessons of experience I need to develop my leadership and management capacity?

- Does this plan include diverse jobs that will stretch my capabilities—jobs where I do not have the answers and where I am required to engage others in problem solving?

- Am I working for a higher-ambition company with the right types of colleagues and a strong performance culture? If not, how can I find such a company, join it, and learn?

- Am I finding ways to exercise my capacity to be honest with myself and with others and to take responsibility for my actions? Am I discovering what makes this difficult for me?

ENGAGE IN HONEST CONVERSATIONS

- Do I ask for and receive honest feedback? Have I developed the trusted relationships with peers, coaches, and bosses to give me this feedback?

A Higher Ambition
for Business

MOST ORGANIZATIONS, in our experience, are able to realize only a small fraction of their potential. They leave much of the energy and talent of their people untapped. A large measure of the human energy they do unleash is dissipated in organizational friction, whether within individual work units, vertically across layers of management, or horizontally across functional, business, or geographic boundaries.

Despite dramatic gains in information processing and communications technology over the past two decades, the gap between performance and potential, in our observation, is actually enlarging. Growth in scale, global reach, business scope, and knowledge intensity is increasing overall organizational diversity and complexity. Simultaneously, the strengthening market for corporate control and the intensifying pressures for short-term results have made managers more inclined to do what is expedient rather than in the long-run interest of the institution.

The CEOs we have described in this book are bucking these trends. They have been crafting a way to lead and manage that, even in the face of these pressures, can achieve superior results in both economic and social terms. Their simultaneous embrace of these dual objectives is precisely why they are able to succeed. By attending seriously to the social dimension, they can create an organizational model that is both "higher energy" and "lower friction," which allows them to succeed in economic terms. By succeeding in creating economic value, they can invest over time in ways that deliver win-win outcomes to all their key stakeholders and sustain the institution's social fabric.

Let us recap the highlights of this higher-energy, lower-friction model.

Higher energy. In chapter 3, we described how higher-ambition CEOs are able to forge a strategic identity for the company that creates greater meaning for people in their work and that keeps them connected with the company's core values and heritage. In chapter 4, we then described how these leaders are able to build energy and excitement about achieving performance excellence. In chapter 5, we saw that being part of a community of shared purpose can create a connection to peers and a sense of personal respect that enable people to bring their whole selves to work. In chapter 6, we highlighted how clarity of priorities and sustained focus create a context for individual initiative. Finally, in chapter 7 we saw how the strong commitment of higher-ambition CEOs *to* the development of down-the-line leaders creates, in turn, a higher level of commitment from these individuals to the long term success of the institution.

Lower friction. In response to the typical dysfunctions in vertical relationships—conflicting priorities, inconsistent resource allocation, sandbagging of budget targets, routinized performance reviews, and constricted upward communication—these CEOs and their organizations spend a disproportionate amount of time: making the direction and priorities clear and consistent; instilling an approach to performance management that shifts the balance from external controls and extrinsic rewards to harness greater levels of peer- and self-governance; and creating channels for vertical communication that increase ongoing learning. In chapter 5 we saw that, in response to the typical challenges in collaborating horizontally across functions, geographies, and other boundaries, these leaders create a community of purpose out of diversity, reduce horizontal friction, and increase the capacity to manage conflict productively. In chapter 6, we noted the emphasis on fairness and inclusion of key stakeholders in difficult decisions. In chapter 7, we saw how the level of the CEOs' personal investment in aligning their senior team and in addressing conflicts directly can enable more unified leadership from the top, reinforced and amplified through an extended leadership group woven together and aligned through a network of personal relationships and high levels of involvement. In essence, these CEOs are creating higher trust systems; trust, in turn, is a huge contributor to reduced friction.

Realizing the Organization's Full Potential

The process of building a higher-ambition institution is an organic, fluid process informed by ongoing organizational and individual learning. The leaders profiled in this book constantly sought to develop the enterprise, to help it evolve and become a higher-ambition firm, just as they themselves grew and deepened their understanding of what they were trying to do and how to do it.

Thirty years ago, the quality movement overturned the prevailing wisdom that cost and quality were trade-offs. Through a different approach to management, the quality movement was able to close the gap between reality and potential performance and demonstrate that "quality is free." By eliminating waste—the hidden costs of nonquality—quality management could deliver superior performance on multiple dimensions simultaneously: quality, cost, and time.

Higher-ambition CEOs, we assert, are demonstrating something comparable in the realm of *leadership*. Through integrated, mutually reinforcing principles and practices, they are showing an ability to realize more of the organization's full potential. Where quality management was concerned with meeting a predefined standard, higher-ambition leadership raises aspirations and defines new possibilities, beyond any benchmark. Just as eliminating waste enables greater quality, faster cycle time, and lower cost, so higher ambition leadership enables superior performance on both economic and social dimensions through greater energy and reduced organizational "friction."

We see these CEOs as part of a vanguard that offers a fundamentally better way to lead large, global, complex institutions in the twenty-first century. As we noted in the introduction, the CEOs we spoke with continue a long tradition of institution builders—such as David Packard and Bill Hewlett at HP; Herb Kelleher of Southwest Airlines; and Matsushita Konosuke, founder of Panasonic, among others—who saw profit as an outcome of good management, as opposed to the sole goal of business. The contribution of the leaders in this study is that they have found a way—a set of principles and practices—that enables successful institution building even in the face of headwinds from capital markets, rapidly changing technology, and unrelenting global competition from sources not experienced or envisioned by institution-builders of the past. We also found that these principles and practices apply for a wide range of businesses and across a spectrum of industries, whether based in India, Europe, or the United States.

We do not claim that these CEOs have perfected this leadership approach, nor that it is sufficient to ensure sustained success. These leaders would be the first to point out the relentless challenges of market dynamics, technological discontinuities, and competitor initiatives.

But we do assert that the world would be a better place if more CEOs led firms in this way. We believe that business institutions play a fundamental role in ensuring that our societies are both prosperous and healthy, creating both economic and social value. The CEOs we interviewed revalidated the vision of Edwin Gay, founding dean of the Harvard Business School; the purpose of business, he believed, is to do "well and good." A century later, we believe this vision still holds.

Leif Johansson elaborated on one particularly distinctive contribution that companies can make to society:

> Name any nationality, any background, any religion—we have them at Volvo. We see them and treat them as colleagues. We, as companies, have a great opportunity to contribute to the development of societies, because we have a much simpler case of integration than most societies do and most political leaders are faced with. We have a really good way of measuring whether we actually succeed at working in a diverse group. And we can celebrate our success, or we can say we did not succeed.

In that way, as Johansson suggests, corporations can help build a global community.

What Can Be Done?

Our focus throughout this book has been on the leader, in the belief that many more leaders could and would choose to pursue this approach if they could clearly see their way to doing so. For these practices to become the norm, however—both accepted and expected—substantial changes need to occur in two other relevant arenas: boards of directors and business schools. Additionally, measures that encourage shareholders to take a long-term perspective on value creation could potentially accelerate the shift.

Reconceive the Role of the Board of Directors

Many of the leaders in our study highlighted the importance of their relationship with the board of directors to their efforts in building a sustainable institution. In most cases, the CEOs felt fortunate to have supportive boards, which understood and embraced the long-term, transformative nature of their leadership task. When CEOs had taken dramatic, bet-the-company moves (for example, Sands and Davies' Christmas-time acquisition of Korea First Bank), they spoke of tight alignment with the board as a critical enabler.

However, we would observe that many CEOs are not this fortunate. We have seen too many instances where the board's predominant focus on financial returns or loss of nerve in the face of predatory hedge-fund share purchases derailed the CEO's institution-building work or, in the extreme, led to the CEO's ouster, despite a strong multiyear track record of improving performance and transforming the company's culture.

We think fundamental change in the role and work of the board is needed if higher-ambition leadership is to become the norm. The failures of companies like Lehman Brothers, Bear Stearns, and Country Mutual during the economic meltdown of 2008, and Enron and WorldCom a decade earlier, point to an uncomfortable truth: boards do not pay sufficient attention to the CEO's values and purpose or the kind of institution their CEO is building.

Based on our research and work with a variety of companies, we believe that boards must more consistently:[1]

- Hold CEOs accountable for achieving short-term performance targets in a way that builds long-term success, and develop a strong social institution that delivers value to all stakeholders, not just the shareholder.

- Insist that their CEO and top team, working in partnership with them, articulate a higher purpose and related performance goals, and a set of values that provides a fundamental compass to ensure that the enterprise stays on track. Too many boards restrict their work to financial reviews and acquisitions and not to strategy and, in particular, purpose and values.

- Manage CEO succession with explicit attention to candidates' capacity for providing higher-ambition leadership.

- Provide oversight of how effectively the purpose, goals, and values are realized throughout the organization. This requires the adoption of what Mike Beer has called a "learning and governance process" that ensures transparency and voice from deep in the organization.[2] For example, as we have seen, Becton Dickinson's Ludwig has repeatedly used a team of high potential employees to learn about his organization and culture. He has also voluntarily shared the unvarnished truth he learned about his company's strengths and weaknesses with his board members and kept them informed about the progress of the corporate transformation.

Develop an Integrative Curriculum at Business Schools

A degree in business, particularly an MBA, has become a virtual necessity for those seeking a leadership position at the top of any large corporation or an influential position in consulting, investment banking, or private equity.[3] Business schools form the assumptions of their students about the purpose of business and "good" leadership and management practices. Correspondingly, their graduates' practice of management shapes business schools.[4] Rakesh Khurana argues persuasively that the original high aspirations of business school founders like Gay, quoted earlier, are as yet unfulfilled. Management, unlike medicine or the law, has yet to become a profession characterized by standards of practice that are motivated by moral and social purpose; those standards would bring to management and business institutions greater legitimacy in the eyes of society.

It seems clear to us that the leaders in our study have broken free of the assumption, perpetuated by many business schools, that the purpose of business is solely to increase shareholder value. Instead, they have been guided by a vision similar to that of Gay in shaping the development of their own leadership principles and practices.

How should business schools incorporate what our CEOs have learned into their curricula? Unless they redesign their courses, the wisdom our leaders developed is unlikely to become the norm and the schools are unlikely to create higher-ambition leaders in any significant numbers. As the start of a broader discussion and debate on curriculum design, we return to a fundamental principle that we have shown underlies the practice of higher-ambition leaders—*integrity*.

By integrity, we do not mean more courses about right or wrong or the legal sanctions that follow ethically questionable business practices, though these are also important. The integrity that we saw our CEOs display had a lot more to do with integration—the integration of the principles and practices represented by our chapter headings into a coherent, systemic approach to building a higher-ambition company. Starting with the development of the firm's strategic identity, the CEOs proceeded to develop practices for performance management, community building, leadership development, and *sisu* personal leadership that were mutually reinforcing and tied to their fundamental human values. These practices represented an integrated, coherent whole; the CEOs adapted the practices to enable a "simultaneous solve," a way to create both economic and social value. And their own identity as leaders continued to evolve based on self-reflection and the will and skill to learn from their experience. These were not isolated practices developed by the strategy or human resource departments. Their architecture sprang from the leaders themselves.

We observe as teachers and/or former students of business management that most MBA curricula do not integrate the multiple disciplines of management. Courses are stand-alone affairs. Students learn about strategy and finance in isolation from each other and from other courses about operations, organizational behavior, or marketing, for example. When students take a course in leadership or ethics, it is disconnected from courses that teach the hard stuff of finance. What schools need is a curriculum that teaches students these subjects and perspectives in relationship to each other and in the context of building a higher-ambition institution.

Even when business schools attempt to integrate technical subjects, as several have done, that integration is still devoid of a definition of corporate purpose and values, something on which faculty from diverse functional disciplines such as finance and organizational behavior would be hard-pressed to agree. Schools base academic advancement on peer review and recognition, which pushes faculty to become discipline-centric, making it virtually impossible for them to agree on the values and purpose of business and how to integrate and adapt their respective technical subjects to each other. That is the challenge.

Fresh thinking will be required from many quarters. Particularly promising, in our view, is engaging higher-ambition leaders themselves to help reshape business education. Examples are Ken Freeman, former CEO of Quest Diagnostics, as the dean at Boston University's School of Management and Bill George, former CEO of Medtronic, now at Harvard Business School, who has refocused leadership development on student self-reflection and clarification of personal values.

Encourage a Long-Term Shareholder Perspective

Markets are powerful catalysts for economic growth. They release animal spirits that engender entrepreneurship and economic value creation. But, as the economic meltdown of 2008 once again taught us, markets can also encourage speculation and an exclusive focus on short-term gains, while discouraging investment in social value creation. The contribution of the CEOs we profile here is that they found a way to maintain a long-term perspective of investment and institution building in the face of pressures for short-term results.

We would be foolish to believe that the higher-ambition leadership our CEOs demonstrated can become the norm without changes in the context that shapes investor behavior. In a governance model that gives primacy to shareholders, we think it important to find ways to encourage shareholders themselves to take a long-term perspective on value creation. In a thought-provoking study, Danny Miller and Isabelle Le Breton-Miller have shown that family-controlled businesses that take a longer-term shareholder perspective and are less subject to the forces of the market for corporate control outperform public companies in shareholder value creation.[5] They found that one of the main reasons is the greater commitment of the leaders of these businesses to a multi-stakeholder approach and a greater motivation to leave an enduring legacy. The leaders build both economic and social capital, developing stronger long-term relationships with their employees, suppliers, and customers. They also control risk—for example, avoiding too much debt or acquisitions that could jeopardize the firm—yet are able to act decisively at moments of discontinuity. All this is enabled by a shareholder perspective that is strongly weighted to the long term.

In public shareholding contexts, such as in the United States and United Kingdom, where there has been a significant increase in the weight of short-term versus long-term shareholding, we think it critical to examine the issue. We do not offer specific solutions, but encourage research and discussion of potential ideas, such as those proposed by the Aspen Institute's Business and Society Program, that might lengthen the time horizon of investors or increase the voice of long-term shareholders, as a way, in turn, of extending the time horizon of the board and of business leaders.[6]

The focus of this book has been on a distinctive approach to leadership. We learned from CEOs about the aspirations, principles, and practices that, in combination, allowed them to achieve a higher ambition. We were inspired by the leadership stories we heard and believe that employees, investors, customers, communities, and society at large will benefit if more leaders— a significant majority—adopt higher-ambition leadership.

Ultimately, if higher-ambition leadership is to become the norm, societies have to develop the institutional context—standards, structures, policies, incentives, and cultural understandings—that shape leadership and organizational behavior.[7] We urge higher-ambition leaders to help spread their approach, mentor other leaders, and reshape the role of the boards where they have influence; researchers and educators to help develop a deeper understanding of higher-ambition leadership and to use those insights to reshape business education; and policy makers to consider the ways they can help reshape the institutional context.

Afterword

Like the CEOs we profile in this book, we, the coauthors, have a higher ambition. We want to expand the circle of higher-ambition leadership in the world—leaders who are committed to creating superior and lasting economic and social value. We came to this research project with the belief, based on years of research and consulting with some of the world's best firms, that building a great institution whose purpose includes but reaches beyond quarterly earnings and shareholder return is desirable and possible. During the four years we spent interviewing thirty-six CEOs in diverse industries and parts of the world, analyzing the data, and discussing our findings, our convictions have grown stronger, not only about the desirability of building a higher-ambition company, but also about the possibility.

To further that possibility, we have launched the TruePoint Center, a not-for-profit international education and research institute dedicated to the development and dissemination of knowledge about how leaders can better build organizations that excel at creating both economic and social value. The center's mission is to expand the practice of higher-ambition leadership. The center brings together like-minded CEOs and companies from around the world as well as other members of their senior teams and their next-generation leaders in a learning community. TruePoint Center does research on how to lead, design, and develop for-profit and nonprofit institutions that sustainably deliver superior value to all key stakeholders. The center also seeks to develop the next generation of higher-ambition leaders who can carry on the work of building their institutions, something the leaders portrayed in this book spoke about with urgency and passion. The work of the center is described further at www.TruePoint.org.

Appendix
Research Design and Directions for Future Research

The findings in this study are based on interviews and discussions with thirty-six CEOs on three continents (see table I-1)—fifteen in the United States, two in Canada, fifteen in Europe, and four in India. In some cases, their participation included many conversations over a number of years, as well as contributing to several CEO round-table discussion forums that we have hosted; at a minimum, it consisted of a one- to two-hour face-to-face interview.

Sample Selection

Our sample of CEOs is purposive. Initially, we were seeking CEOs who would be thoughtful about the leadership challenges of creating lasting organizations that are high performing and that achieve high levels of commitment from their employees and other key stakeholders. We also wanted to ensure that they had a track record of success in meeting these dual objectives. Thus, at the start of our work, we sought CEOs who were creating both economic value and social *capital.* Over the course of our research, it became clear that the CEOs we were speaking with were concerned not only with creating social capital, but also with explicitly contributing to the social *good.* We therefore broadened the framing to our current formulation of leaders who are creating both economic value and social *value.*

To find these CEOs, we relied on recommendations from trusted colleagues, our own direct experience in working with some of these leaders, as well as the usual lists of most-admired companies and best places to work. As a check on these judgments, we applied two tests:

- The CEO's company must have had a compounded annual growth rate in revenues, profits, and market capitalization that exceeded the fiftieth percentile of industry peers between 1997 and 2006, or for the CEO tenure. Corresponding figures were used for public or privately held organizations.

- There was evidence from the public record—articles, speeches, and views of those with direct knowledge—that the CEO was concerned with developing a people-centric, high-commitment culture.

CEOs who met these criteria received a letter from Professor Mike Beer on Harvard Business School stationery requesting their participation in a study of CEOs who are leading high-commitment, high-performance companies. We then interviewed those CEOs who chose to participate and continued to check for sufficient corroborating evidence to justify inclusion.

Directions for Further Research

By its nature, this study was intended as exploratory research to generate hypotheses about a distinctive model of leadership. It was not designed to test them rigorously, nor to "prove" that leaders who follow the practices described here will necessarily outperform their peers.

Our research sources were the CEOs themselves. While we exercised reasonable diligence to find corroborating external evidence that they were achieving results consistent with the theories they articulated, we do not know the extent of the gap between what these CEOs espouse and what is actually happening across the various parts of their companies. Indeed, we would suggest a fruitful area for further research would be in-depth, in-company research to explore the various aspects of this question: for example, how consistent are these companies in applying the approaches the CEO articulates? Just how different are the internal cultures and the nature of collaboration in these companies from others where CEOs are pursuing a more traditional leadership model? To what extent do these internal differences translate into genuine sources of advantage?

We also cannot be certain of the sustainability of the culture and performance of the companies in this study. Only a longitudinal study would allow us to answer this question. We know from past research and books—*In Search of Excellence, Built to Last,* and *Good to Great,* for example—that exceptional performance or practices do not always last. We expect the same thing will ultimately prove true of the companies in our study. While the leadership approaches described here can be no guarantee of survival, we would predict, however, that they will contribute to resilience, as we saw anecdotally in the case of Standard Chartered Bank's weathering of the global financial crisis. We would therefore encourage further research into whether these leadership practices contribute positively to adaptation, resilience, and renewal, and if so, under what circumstances.

Finally, we do not claim to have provided a definitive articulation of the leadership model we are seeking to describe. We were struck by the consistency in how these CEOs spoke to us about the challenges of leading with a higher ambition and how they thought about the work of leadership itself, despite the widely varying contexts in which they were leading. The remarkable similarity in the principles and practices they described (and how different they were from those of other CEOs we have interviewed or worked with) convinced us that these leaders are converging on a common leadership paradigm. But we would welcome further research beyond the initial sketch we offer here to elaborate the principles and practices that constitute its essence.

Notes

Introduction

1. See for example, Rensis Likert, *The Human Organization: Its Management and Value* (New York: McGraw Hill, 1967); Dan Dennison, *Corporate Culture and Organizational Effectiveness* (New York: Wiley, 1990); John P. Kotter and James L. Heskett, *Corporate Culture and Performance* (New York: Free Press, 1992); Jeffrey Pfeffer, *The Human Equation: Building Profits by Putting People First* (Boston, MA: Harvard Business School Press, 1998); James N. Baron and Michael T. Hannan, "Organizational Blueprints for Success in High-Tech Start-ups: Lessons Learned from the Stanford Project on Emerging Companies," *California Management Review* 44, no. 3 (2002): 8–36.

2. See Michael E. Porter and Mark R. Kramer, "Creating Shared Value," *Harvard Business Review,* January–February 2011, 62–77; Rosabeth Moss Kanter, *SuperCorp: How Vanguard Companies Create Innovation, Profits, Growth and Social Good* (New York: Crown Business, 2009); James Collins and Jerry I. Porras, *Built to Last: Successful Habits of Visionary Companies* (New York: Harper Business, 1991); Thomas J. Peters, *In Search of Excellence: Lessons from America's Best-Run Companies* (New York: Warner Books, 1984); *Good to Great: Why Some Companies Make the Leap . . . and Others Don't* (New York: HarperCollins, 2001).

3. See Michael Beer, *High Commitment, High Performance: How to Build a Resilient Organization for Sustained Advantage* (San Francisco, CA: Jossey-Bass, 2009); Michael Beer, Russell A. Eisenstat, and Bert Spector, *The Critical Path to Corporate Renewal* (Boston: Harvard Business School Press, 1990); Russell Eisenstat, Nathaniel Foote, Jay Galbraith, and Danny Miller, "Beyond the Business Unit," *McKinsey Quarterly,* January 2001, 54–63; Danny Miller, Russell Eisenstat, and Nathaniel Foote, "Strategy from the Inside Out: Building Capability-Creating Organizations," *California Management Review* 44, no. 3 (2002): 37–54.

Chapter 1

1. Louis Lavelle, "What Campbell's New Chief Needs to Do Now," *BusinessWeek,* June 25, 2001, http://www.businessweek.com/magazine/content/01_26/b3738082.htm.

2. Reed Abelson, "The First Family of Soup, Feeling the Squeeze," *New York Times,* July 30, 2000.

3. Russell A. Eisenstat, Michael Beer, Nathaniel Foote, Tobias Fredberg, and Flemming Norrgren, "The Uncompromising Leader," *Harvard Business Review,* July–August 2008, 50–57.

Chapter 3

1. Kevin J. O'Brien, "Nokia's New Chief Faces Culture of Complacency," *New York Times,* September 26, 2010.

2. Though Nokia's global smartphone market share was reported to have declined from 36 percent in 2009 to 29 percent in 2010, it remained the global leader; see Gustav Sandstrom, "3rd Update: Nokia Market Share Slides—Gartner," *Wall Street Journal,* February 9, 2011.

Chapter 4

1. InterOrganization Network's (ION) inaugural list of "Guys Who Get It," a compilation of eleven leading executives at U.S. public companies who recognize the value of diversity; the 2010 Catalyst Award for success in advancing women to leadership roles; the Boston College Center for Corporate Citizenship; and the Reputation Institute's Corporate Social Responsibility Index.

2. John Stackhouse, "The World in 1993: India Stop-and-Go Reform," *Globe and Mail* (Canada), December 18, 1992.

Chapter 5

1. "Heart Principles," Bright Horizons Family Solutions, www.brighthorizons.com.

Chapter 6

1. Randall Rothenberg, "Kenneth W. Freeman: The Thought Leader Interview," *Strategy + Business* 37 (Winter 2004).

2. See Michael Beer and Russell A. Eisenstat, "The Silent Killers of Strategy Implementation," *MIT Sloan Management Review,* Summer 2000, 29–40.

Chapter 8

1. See K. E. Kram and M. C. Higgins, "A New Mindset on Mentoring: Developing Developmental Networks at Work," *Wall Street Journal,* September 2008; *MIT Sloan Management Review,* February 2009.

2. Morgan W. McCall, Michael M. Lombardo, and Ann M. Morrison, *Lessons of Experience: How Executives Develop on the Job* (New York: Free Press, 1988).

3. For more information about the approach Ludwig used to engage his people, see Michael Beer and Russell A. Eisenstat, "How to Have an Honest Conversation about Your Business Strategy," *Harvard Business Review,* February 2004, 82–89.

Chapter 9

1. These ideas are elaborated in Nathaniel Foote and Michael Beer, "The New Governance Paradigm," *Directorship Magazine,* September 2009.

2. See Michael Beer, *High Commitment, High Performance: How to Build a Resilient Organization for Sustained Advantage* (San Francisco: Jossey-Bass, 2009).

3. Rakesh Khurana, *From Higher Aims to Hired Hands: The Social Transformation of American Business Schools and the Unfulfilled Promise of Management as a Profession* (Princeton, NJ: Princeton University Press, 2009), 4.

4. Ibid., 5.

5. Danny Miller and Isabelle Le Breton-Miller, *Managing for the Long Run: Lessons in Competitive Advantage from Great Family Businesses* (Boston: Harvard Business School Press, 2005).

6. The Aspen Institute, Business and Society Program, "Overcoming Short-Termism: A Call for a More Responsible Approach to Investment and Business Management," September 9, 2009.

7. Khurana, *From Higher Aims to Hired Hands*. For an excellent discussion of the relationship between institutions and individuals, in the context of the role of business schools, see the introduction.

Index

Acknowledgments

The CEOs we spoke to repeatedly stressed the collective nature of higher-ambition leadership. This was certainly true of the creation of this book: the research and writing was a collective effort that extends well beyond the five authors.

First, without the investment of time by the CEOs we interviewed and their open sharing of their hard-won insights and wisdom, this book would not have been possible. While some of the CEOs and their stories feature more prominently in the text, the findings are based on a thorough analysis and weighting of the perspectives of all the CEOs in the study. We appreciate the generosity of spirit with which the CEOs engaged with us throughout the project.

A number of our colleagues helped us conduct interviews with higher-ambition leaders, including Kathy MacDonald, Chris Richmond, Derek Schrader, and Dick Shafer. Malcolm Wolf and Ravi Venkatesan took the lead on our four interviews with Indian CEOs. Thomas Rice partnered with Mike Beer to conduct a round of follow-up interviews with a few of our CEOs that focused on their development as leaders. These interviews and Thomas's insights greatly enriched the themes and content of chapter 8, "Becoming a Higher-Ambition Leader."

The quality of this manuscript has also benefited greatly from the comments and reflections of our editor at the Harvard Business Review Press, Melinda Merino, and of other close colleagues, including Niclas Adler, Jim Bennett, Maria Elmquist, Magnus Finnström, Björn Frössevi, Jay Galbraith, Ola Jönsson, Kathrin Möslein, Hannes Norrrgren, Marcus Norrgren, Sean Quigley, Shankar Raman, Chris Richmond, Dick Shafer, and Ravi Venkatesan. They repeatedly challenged us to sharpen our thinking and clarify our language, reminding us that the topic was just too important to not get right. Special thanks are owed to one of our higher-ambition leaders, Peter Dunn, for his thorough review and insightful comments on an earlier draft of this manuscript. Likewise, Peter Lundin, a higher-ambition leader not included in the sample, provided valuable feedback on early drafts.

This book would not have come to life without the patience and extraordinary craft of our collaborating writer, John Butman, and his colleagues, Hannah Alpert-Abrams and Anna Weiss. We are grateful to them for successfully taking on the quixotic task of working with five very opinionated coauthors and helping us to create an integrated manuscript that represents the best of all of us. We are also deeply appreciative of the extensive support we received from our colleagues at TruePoint. The patience, good humor, and enthusiasm they have shown over the four years it has taken for this work to come to fruition are only exceeded by that shown by our families.

The Division of Research at Harvard Business School provided funding for our analysis to select the sample, for transcription, and for three conferences in the United States at which we shared preliminary findings from this research with over thirty higher-ambition leaders and benefited from their perspectives. Chalmers University provided equivalent support for a similar conference held in Sweden. At Chalmers, Dean Per Svensson and Research Division head Mats Lundqvist have provided Flemming and Tobias time, financial support, leeway in their academic duties, and collegial understanding for this very time-consuming project. In the Division for the Management of Organizational Renewal and Entrepreneurship, our close colleague Susanne Ollila has been a continuous source of encouragement throughout this period. Christopher Hedvall needs a warm and special thanks for his great work managing some of the extensive data that we collected, as does Clara Strömbeck for her quick, accurate help at the end of this writing period. Tobias is very grateful to the Tom Hedelius and Jan Wallander Foundation for a research stipend that made the first year of this research possible, and for a travel grant that funded a period as guest researcher at Harvard Business School to focus on the writing of this book. We are grateful to Karin Nilsson and Jan Simmons for the unfailing grace and competence with which they supported the complex administrative requirements of this project—from arranging the logistics of interviews, to transcribing interviews, to ensuring that the four conferences we conducted came off without a hitch.

Finally, we have listed the names of the coauthors alphabetically on the title page because this book was the result of a team effort with five equally contributing members. The coauthors and John Butman spent many days discussing and analyzing the meaning of our interviews. Out of these discussions, the key themes in this book emerged. We each then took responsibility for writing up the first drafts of the individual chapters and then worked together to sharpen the content and weave together key themes. We chose to highlight two members of the author team, Mike Beer and Flemming Norrgren, on the front cover of this book because they will be playing a leading role in taking this work forward in their respective roles as the chairman of the TruePoint Center and director of the TruePoint Center Europe.

About the Authors

MICHAEL BEER is the Cahners Rabb Professor of Business Administration, Emeritus, at Harvard Business School; Chairman of TruePoint Center, a not-for-profit research and education organization; and Chairman of TruePoint Partners, an international consulting firm. Before joining HBS, Mike founded and served as Director of the Organizational Research and Development Department at Corning, Inc. Mike is the recipient of numerous professional honors and awards, including the Academy of Management's Distinguished Scholar-Practitioner Award, the Society of Industrial and Organizational Psychology's Distinguished Professional Contributions Award, and the Michael R. Losey Research Award from the Society for Human Resource Management. He has authored eleven books, including *High Commitment, High Performance: How to Build a Resilient Organization for Sustained Advantage* (San Francisco: Jossey-Bass, 2009), and written numerous book chapters and articles in academic and business journals.

RUSSELL EISENSTAT is President of TruePoint Partners and a former faculty member at Harvard Business School. Before founding TruePoint with Mike Beer, he was a Senior Organizational Fellow at McKinsey & Co. Russ's areas of expertise include the management of large-scale organizational change and innovation, strategy implementation, and the design of complex organizations. Russ has supported the senior executives of numerous leading corporations in taking their businesses to higher levels of performance, organizational capability, and commitment. Together with Mike Beer and Bert Spector, he is the author of *The Critical Path to Corporate Renewal* (Boston: Harvard Business School Press, 1990), which won the

Johnson, Smith & Kinsley Award for the best book that year on executive leadership. Russ's other writings include "The Uncompromising Leader" and "How to Have an Honest Conversation About Your Business Strategy," both in *Harvard Business Review*, and "The Silent Killers of Strategy Implementation & Learning" in the MIT *Sloan Management Review*.

NATHANIEL FOOTE is Managing Director of TruePoint Partners. Prior to joining TruePoint, Nathaniel spent 19 years with McKinsey & Co. in roles that included leading McKinsey's Organization Design practice, serving as Director of Knowledge and Practice Development, and leading the European Organization practice as a partner in the London office. Nathaniel earned joint degrees from Harvard Law School and Harvard Business School, where he was a Baker Scholar. In his consulting and research, Nathaniel has focused on how adaptive, iterative approaches to strategy, organization design, and knowledge management help complex businesses perform amidst rapid change. He has written numerous articles, such as "Beyond the Business Unit" and "Making Solutions the Answer" in *The McKinsey Quarterly* and "Strategy from the Inside Out" in the *California Management Review*.

TOBIAS FREDBERG is Associate Professor of Management at Chalmers University of Technology in Gothenburg, Sweden, and a Fellow of the TruePoint Center. Tobias was trained in journalism and international business and earned his PhD in technology management from Chalmers. Tobias has been a visiting scholar at the Technische Universität München and at Harvard Business School. His research focuses on leading strategic change and on the management of innovation in highly complex organizations. He currently heads two large research projects in those areas and coleads an international research network. He has written numerous articles, including "The Uncompromising Leader" in *Harvard Business Review* and "Organizing Customers: Learning from Big Brother" in *Long Range Planning*.

FLEMMING NORRGREN is Professor of Management at Chalmers University of Technology, a Partner in TruePoint, and Director of the TruePoint Center in Europe. He earned his PhD in organizational psychology from the University of Gothenburg. Flemming has spent nearly three decades developing managers' skills, building industrial R&D functions, and coordinating large international R&D projects in pharmaceutical, technology, and other knowledge-intensive industries. He has led three major research centers for change management, industrial R&D management, project management, leadership, and socio-technical systems design involving leading companies such as AstraZeneca, Ericsson, and Volvo. He is the author of numerous books and articles and a coauthor of "The Uncompromising Leader," published in *Harvard Business Review*.